Green Thumbs: RADISHES

with paper towels, milk cartons,
foil, tape, jars and simple things

FOUR TEST ENVIRONMENTS IN ONE BABY FOOD JAR!

Tropical

Desert

Cooled
(by evaporation)

Swamp

SCIENCE WITH SIMPLE THINGS SERIES

Conceived and
written by
RON MARSON

Illustrated by
PEG MARSON

TOPS LEARNING SYSTEMS

10970 S Mulino Road
Canby OR 97013
Website: topscience.org
Fax: 1 (503) 266-5200

Oh, those pesky COPYRIGHT RESTRICTIONS!

Dear Educator,

TOPS is a nonprofit organization dedicated to educational ideals, not our bottom line. We have invested much time, energy, money, and love to bring you this excellent teaching resource.

And we have carefully designed this book to run on simple materials you already have or can easily purchase. If you consider the depth and quality of this curriculum amortized over years of teaching, it is dirt cheap, orders of magnitude less than prepackaged kits and textbooks.

Please honor our copyright restrictions. We are a very small company, and book sales are our life blood. When you buy this book and use it for your own teaching, you sustain our publishing effort. If you give or "loan" this book or copies of our lessons to other teachers, with no compensation to TOPS, you squeeze us financially, and may drive us out of business. Our well-being rests in your hands.

What if you are excited about the terrific ideas in this book, and want to share them with your colleagues? What if the teacher down the hall, or your homeschooling neighbor, is begging you for good science, quick! We have suggestions. Please see our *Purchase and Royalty Options* below.

We are grateful for the work you are doing to help shape tomorrow. We are honored that you are making TOPS a part of your teaching effort. Thank you for your good will and kind support.

Sincerely, *Ron Marson*

Purchase and Royalty Options:

Individual teachers, homeschoolers, libraries:

PURCHASE option: If your colleagues are asking to borrow your book, please ask them to read this copyright page, and to contact TOPS for our current catalog so they can purchase their own book. We also have an **online catalog** that you can access at www.topscience.org.

If you are reselling a **used book** to another classroom teacher or homeschooler, please be aware that this still affects us by eliminating a potential book sale. We do not push "newer and better" editions to encourage consumerism. So we ask seller or purchaser (or both!) to acknowledge the ongoing value of this book by sending a contribution to support our continued work. Let your conscience be your guide.

Honor System ROYALTIES: If you wish to make copies from a library, or pass on copies of just a few activities in this book, please calculate their value at 50 cents (25 cents for homeschoolers) per lesson per recipient. Send that amount, or ask the recipient to send that amount, to TOPS. We also gladly accept donations. We know life is busy, but please do follow through on your good intentions promptly. It will only take a few minutes, and you'll know you did the right thing!

Schools and Districts:

You may wish to use this curriculum in several classrooms, in one or more schools. Please observe the following:

PURCHASE option: Order this book in quantities equal to the number of target classrooms. If you order 5 books, for example, then you have unrestricted use of this curriculum in any 5 classrooms per year for the life of your institution. You may order at these quantity discounts:

2-9 copies: 90% of current catalog price + shipping.

10+ copies: 80% of current catalog price + shipping.

ROYALTY option: Purchase 1 book *plus* photocopy or printing rights in quantities equal to the number of designated classrooms. If you pay for 5 Class Licenses, for example, then you have purchased reproduction rights for any 5 classrooms per year for the life of your institution.

1-9 Class Licenses: 70% of current book price per classroom.

10+ Class Licenses: 60% of current book price per classroom.

Workshops and Training Programs:

We are grateful to all of you who spread the word about TOPS. Please limit duplication to only those lessons you will be using, and collect all copies afterward. No take-home copies, please. Copies of copies are prohibited. Ask us for a free shipment of as many current **TOPS Ideas** catalogs as you need to support your efforts. Every catalog contains numerous free sample teaching ideas.

ISBN 0-941008-70-3

CONTENTS

PART I — PREPARATION AND SUPPORT

PART II — ACTIVITIES AND LESSON NOTES

PART III — SUPPLEMENTARY CUTOUT

Getting Ready

Welcome to **Green Thumbs: Radishes.** *Here is a checklist of things to think about and preparations to make before beginning your first lesson.*

✔ Review the scope and sequence.

Take just a few minutes, right now, to thumb through all 20 activity pages. Pause to scan each lesson, then read each *Objective* that begins the accompanying teaching notes.

✔ Set aside appropriate class time.

Consult your school calendar. Block out 4 full weeks of school beginning on a Monday. If your schedule doesn't allow that many continuous days without interruptions or vacations, consult the Master Schedule on page D to devise ways of working around any discontinuity. Allow at least 1 period per school day (50 minutes) for radish activities; ideally even more time for younger students.

Don't teach *Radishes* on alternating M-W-F or Tu-Th schedules. There is too much to do, to observe and to record. If you have an alternating science schedule, consider rearranging it: teach science daily for 4 weeks at the expense of some other subject; then make up that lost subject by teaching it at the expense of science over a similar period.

✔ Evaluate your indoor growing conditions.

Radishes are well suited to the classroom environment, *if* you provide them with basic necessities:

• **LIGHT**: Full-spectrum daylight entering your room through the windows will grow healthy radishes. Narrow-spectrum fluorescent lighting lacks some wavelengths needed for normal photosynthesis.

If your room is not flooded by daylight, your students can still study radishes with the help of supplemental lighting. A variety of portable full-spectrum and "plant" lights are available. Even a couple of desk or table lamps with regular incandescent bulbs will help provide the warm tones missing from the fluorescent lighting in most school rooms. If you use such supplemental lighting, the plants closest to it will benefit the most. Either ask your young botanists to take turns placing their plants near the lights, or have them observe, over time, the differences in plant growth and color.

Radishes, of course, also benefit from direct exposure to sunlight. But this is not a requirement. In fact, unless carefully monitored, direct sunlight can do radishes more harm than good, as they prefer relatively cool temperatures and can't tolerate drying out.

• **SPACE TO GROW**: Radishes don't require much room. Nevertheless, when you multiply the milk carton and baby food jars needed in this unit by all the lab groups that require similar materials, space does become an important consideration.

Fortunately, you don't need gigantic window sills running the length of your room. A couple of large, flat table surfaces will suffice. Each lab group needs a surface area of 1.3 square feet (as large as 2 sheets of notebook paper laid side by side).

If space is tight, use masking tape to subdivide your table tops and shelves into assigned storage areas. Identify each area with tape name tags.

• **WATER**: If you don't have running water in your room, use a pitcher or a gallon plastic milk jug. Provide any small container – cups will do – for carrying water to the radishes. Our Master Schedule contains watering reminders throughout.

✔ Organize a way to track completed work.

Keep completed assignments on file in your classroom. If you lack a file cabinet, a box with a brick will serve. File folders or notebooks make suitable assignment organizers. Students will gain a sense of accomplishment as they see their folders grow heavy, or their notebooks fill, with completed assignments. Reference and review are facilitated, since all papers stay in one place.

Ask students to tape a copy of the Master Schedule (page D) inside the front cover of their folders or notebooks. They can track assignments and you can monitor progress by observing which boxes have been initialed or checked.

✔ Photocopy sets of student activity sheets.

This book contains 22 line masters to photocopy.
• Four of these pages require 1 copy per lab group: Activities 1, 2 and 9; Drawing Grid.
• All remaining 18 pages require 1 copy per student: Master Schedule; Activities 3-8, 10-20.

✔ Assign lab groups.

You can cut space requirements in half by assigning students to work in pairs. Two is better than three; fewer hands result in more involvement. Two is also better than one. If one student is absent, the second can work alone, keeping pace with the growing radishes.

Consider which students work most cooperatively together. Avoid pairing dominant and passive students. Lab partners will share lab materials and work cooperatively on experiments. But all activity pages requiring written responses should still be completed by each individual.

✔ Collect needed materials.

See page B, opposite, for details.

Gathering Materials

Listed below is everything you'll need to teach this unit. Buy what you don't already have from your local supermarket, drugstore or hardware store. Ask students to bring recycled materials from home.

Keep this classification key in mind as you review what's needed.

general on-the-shelf materials: Normal type suggests that these materials are used often. Keep these basics on shelves or in drawers that are readily accessible to your students. The next TOPS unit you teach will likely utilize many of these same materials.	*special in-a-box materials:* Italic type suggests that these materials are unusual. Keep these specialty items in a separate box. After you finish teaching this unit, label the box for storage and put it away, ready to use again.
(substituted materials): Parentheses enclosing any item suggests a ready substitute. These alternatives may work just as well as the original. Don't be afraid to improvise, to make do with what you have.	***optional materials:** An asterisk sets these items apart. They are nice to have, but you can easily live without them. They are probably not worth an extra trip to the store, unless you are gathering other materials as well.

Everything is listed in order of first use. Start gathering at the top of this list and work down. Ask students to bring recycled items from home. The Teaching Notes may occasionally suggest additional *Extensions*. Materials for these optional experiments are listed neither here nor under *Materials*. Read the extension itself to determine what new items, if any, are required.

Quantities depend on how many students you have, how you organize them into activity groups, and how you teach. Decide which of these estimates best applies to you, then adjust quantities up or down as necessary:

Q_1/Q_2

Single Student: Enough for 1 student to do all the experiments.

Classroom: Enough for 30 students when organized into 15 lab pairs.

KEY:	*special in-a-box materials* (substituted materials)	general on-the-shelf materials *optional materials

1/15	cardboard milk cartons, half gallon size
1/15	pairs scissors, some heavy duty — see teaching notes 1
1/3	rolls masking tape
1/3	rolls soft, absorbent paper towels
1/15	ballpoint pens
1/3	*one-gallon plastic milk jugs for watering (pitchers)
1/2	*packets radish seeds, 4 to 5 grams each*
1/30	*file folders (notebooks)
1/2	rolls aluminum foil
2/30	index cards, 4 x 6 inch size
1/15	size-D batteries — dead or alive
1/3	rolls transparent tape — matte surface for writing on (masking tape)
1/6	*quarts potting soil*
1/15	styrofoam trays — see teaching notes 2
1/30	sharp pencils with soft, clean erasers
5/75	baby food jars with lids — assorted sizes OK
1/1	roll plastic wrap
2/30	paper clips
1/15	jars — pint or quart, with lids
1/1	box table salt
1/1	bottle vinegar
1/5	glasses (beakers)
1/5	teaspoons
1/15	*hand lenses

Sequencing Activities

Radishes develop by their own timetable. Their fast growth cycle makes them wonderful subjects for all kinds of classroom investigation. But their speed brings potential problems, too. If you observe them for a lab period, nothing much appears to happen. But if you leave for the weekend, then look again on Monday, what you hoped to see on Friday may already be done and gone.

To study radishes successfully in the classroom, important growing events must occur on weekdays. You must start experiments on a day that will create a future window of opportunity to observe, on a school day, what may be a fleeting event in the life of a radish. You must do activities in a specific order. Fail to start one on time, or do it out of sequence, and the resulting disturbance will ripple through related activities.

Can you keep your science class in step with radishes? Sure you can! **We've done the planning for you.** Follow the calendar of events on the opposite page, and stay reasonably on schedule.

But what if you teach science only 3 days a week? Or what if your calendar has a hole in it, say an in-service day a week from Friday? Unfortunately, radishes develop too rapidly to be observed only every other day. We hope you can avoid serious interruptions, or plan around them. Changing your teaching schedule is considerably easier than changing the way radishes grow!

If you must deviate from this calendar, please do so thoughtfully. Look under Scheduling in the teaching notes if you anticipate that a day's activity needs to be moved up or back. This section tells you how each activity is related to all the rest, so you can see where problems will most likely occur. You'll also learn when it's OK to get a bit ahead of schedule, or to fall a little behind.

Snow days or flu epidemics are potential problems. What if both members of a lab group miss critical observations? Ask them to review the results of other groups that recorded data accurately, and write a report hypothesizing what their own plants were doing during that time period, complete with extrapolated graphs or drawings. And it's possible, of course, to drop one or two experiments completely, and still offer your students a rich learning experience.

Notice the large and small boxes on the Master Schedule. Each activity has a large checkoff box. A large box means that particular activity, which may have been partially done on previous days, is finished. We recommend that you initial these large boxes yourself as a final teacher-check. A small box means the activity page is still in progress. Students should check off these small boxes themselves as they finish each day's work. In this way you can tell at a glance who is on track and who requires extra supervision.

Hmmm ~ Friday of week 3 would fall on an inservice day...

... we'd miss a day of data collection for our Activity 20 graphs, but we can squeeze Activity 19 in on Monday. I think we can live with that...

MASTER SCHEDULE

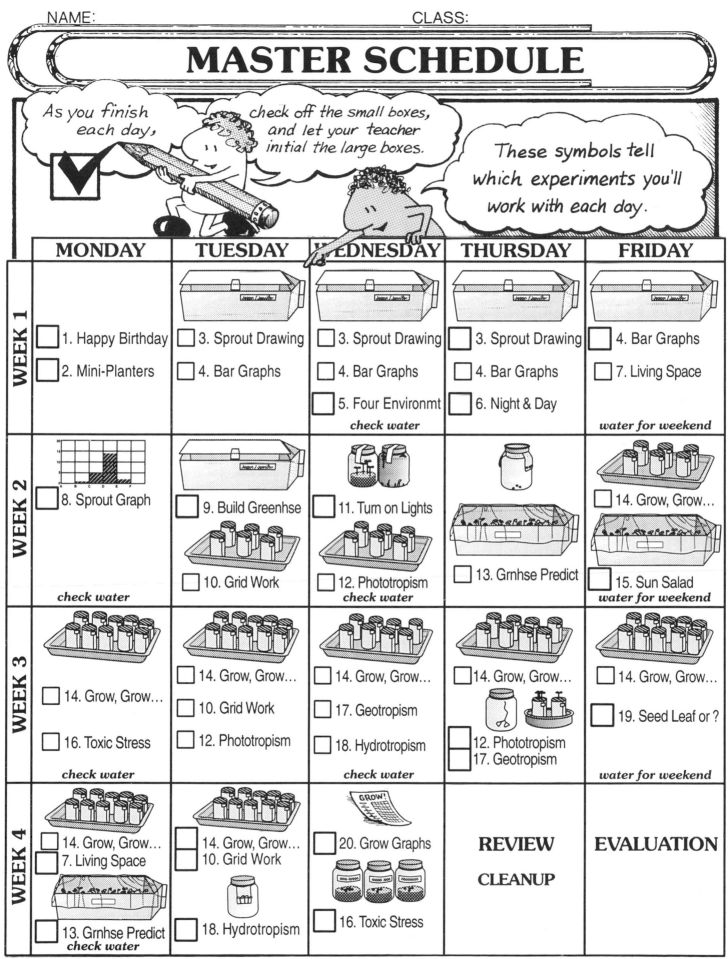

As you finish each day,

check off the small boxes, and let your teacher initial the large boxes.

These symbols tell which experiments you'll work with each day.

	MONDAY	TUESDAY	WEDNESDAY	THURSDAY	FRIDAY
WEEK 1	1. Happy Birthday 2. Mini-Planters	3. Sprout Drawing 4. Bar Graphs	3. Sprout Drawing 4. Bar Graphs 5. Four Environmt *check water*	3. Sprout Drawing 4. Bar Graphs 6. Night & Day	4. Bar Graphs 7. Living Space *water for weekend*
WEEK 2	8. Sprout Graph *check water*	9. Build Greenhse 10. Grid Work	11. Turn on Lights 12. Phototropism *check water*	13. Grnhse Predict	14. Grow, Grow… 15. Sun Salad *water for weekend*
WEEK 3	14. Grow, Grow… 16. Toxic Stress *check water*	14. Grow, Grow… 10. Grid Work 12. Phototropism	14. Grow, Grow… 17. Geotropism 18. Hydrotropism *check water*	14. Grow, Grow… 12. Phototropism 17. Geotropism	14. Grow, Grow… 19. Seed Leaf or ? *water for weekend*
WEEK 4	14. Grow, Grow… 7. Living Space 13. Grnhse Predict *check water*	14. Grow, Grow… 10. Grid Work 18. Hydrotropism	20. Grow Graphs 16. Toxic Stress	**REVIEW** **CLEANUP**	**EVALUATION**

D

TOPS LEARNING SYSTEMS

Review / Test Questions

Photocopy the test questions below. Cut out those you wish to use, and tape them onto white paper. Include questions of your own design, as well. Crowd them all onto a single page for students to answer on their own papers, or leave space for student responses after each question, as you wish. Duplicate a class set, and your custom-made test is ready to use. Use leftover questions as a class review in preparation for the final exam.

activity 1-4 A
Label the parts of this radish seed and seedling.

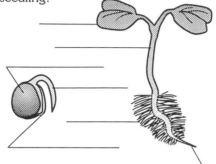

activity 3
In a tropical jungle you discover a small rare plant, that no scientist has previously documented (drawn or described). You wish to make an enlarged drawing of this small wonder, sketching its proportions as accurately as you can. How will you do it?

activity 1-4 B
A radish seed finds itself in a warm, moist environment. Describe its development during the first 5 days. Write complete sentences using your own words. Use accurate, well-labeled diagrams.

activity 5
Name 3 things radish seeds need in order to sprout.

activity 6
What does a scientist do when she predicts?

activity 7
Directions on a radish seed package tell you to thin the young seedlings to 5 cm apart in the row. Won't pulling out radishes just reduce your crop? Explain.

activity 8
A tree is losing its leaves as winter approaches. Explain how this process fits a sigma curve. Illustrate your answer with a graph.

activity 9
Why is putting a clear plastic cover over your greenhouse helpful to your radish seedlings?

activity 10
Label the parts of this 3-week old radish.

activity 11
An empty box has been laying in a grassy field for several weeks, open side down. If you lift it up and peek underneath, predict what you might see.

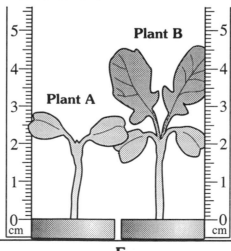

activity 12
You are growing house plants next to a window. To make these plants grow straight, you need to turn them every few days. Explain why this is necessary.

activity 13
A package of seeds says "store in a cool, dry place." Why is this good advice?

activity 14
Give the height of each plant to the nearest 0.1 cm.

Plant B

Plant A

activity 15
Explain how radishes help your body use the sun as an energy source.

activity 16
You suspect water pollution is adversely affecting your crops. Design an experiment to test your hypothesis.

activity 17
Do you think that plants grown under weightless conditions in a space greenhouse would develop an earth-like appearance? Explain.

activity 18
You have a potted plant that can be watered from above, or from a saucer at the base. Where should you water daily in order to develop the deepest root system? Explain.

activity 19
A. What would happen to a newly sprouted radish seedling without cotyledons? Explain.
B. What would happen to a radish plant without leaves? Explain.

activity 20
Height measurements were taken of two radishes over a period of 1 week. Which one is the older radish? Explain how you know.

	RADISH #1 (cm)	RADISH #2 (cm)
SUNDAY	8.3	6.5
MONDAY	8.5	7.1
TUESDAY	8.7	7.9
WEDNESDAY	8.8	8.9
THURSDAY	8.9	9.9
FRIDAY	9.0	10.7
SATURDAY	9.0	11.3

E

Answers

activity 1-4 A

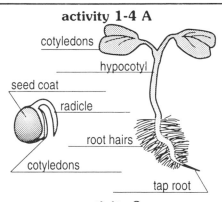

cotyledons

hypocotyl

seed coat

radicle

root hairs

cotyledons

tap root

activity 3

Prepare 2 grids, one with smaller and the other with larger squares. Number or letter the columns and rows of each grid in the same manner. Place the small grid behind the plant, then draw it square for square onto the larger grid.

activity 1-4 B

This question challenges students to summarize a whole week of radish observations into an organized report. They should present information and drawings that are similar (but not identical) to Growth Stages A through F detailed in activity 3. Allow time for students to make their best effort. Evaluate output in terms of accuracy, effort and originality.

activity 5

(1) water   (2) free oxygen   (3) warmth

activity 6

She makes an educated guess as to how an experiment will turn out before it happens, based on available information. (This is also called an hypothesis.)

activity 7

Thinning radishes gives each plant more growing space, and less competition for water, light and nutrients. This practice actually increases yield. You get fewer radishes, but those will grow much larger.

activity 8

The tree loses leaves slowly at first, then more and more rapidly as winter approaches. As this process continues, there are fewer and fewer leaves left on the tree to fall off. So the whole process slows down until the tree is almost bare, dropping only an occasional leaf.

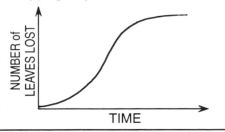

activity 9

The clear plastic lets in light and slows the loss of water by evaporation, thus warming the growing environment a bit. All these effects benefit the radish seedlings.

activity 10

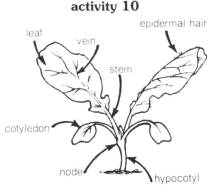

leaf

vein

stem

epidermal hair

cotyledon

node

hypocotyl

activity 11

The grass under the box would probably look yellow and tall. Without light, it can't make green chlorophyll. In darkness its cells would elongate, increasing the possibility that the grass might grow into life-sustaining light.

activity 12

Green plants are phototropic. They grow toward the dominant light source, in this case a window. Rotating them, in effect, causes this window light to fall equally on all sides, so they will not lean in any favored direction.

activity 13

A seed lives in a slow-motion state of suspended animation. Moisture and warmth, though not enough to cause sprouting, stimulate the metabolic draw on its food reserves, thus reducing its overall life span. By keeping seeds in a cool, dry place, you minimize the rate of metabolism, and thus maximize the period of viability.

activity 14

Plant A: 2.9 cm   **Plant B:** 4.6 cm

activity 15

Sunlight falls onto green radish leaves. The chlorophyll in these leaves uses the sun's energy to photosynthesize sugars. The radish transfers these sugars to the hypocotyl for storage. Now I eat this hypocotyl. My body burns the sugar in this radish, converting it back to energy — energy that originated in the sun.

activity 16

Grow 2 batches of crops. Water one batch with local water that you suspect is polluted. Water the other with a source that you know is pure. Compare the growth of crops in both batches.

activity 17

Not likely. On Earth, geotropisms give the plant an orderly appearance. The shoot grow up and the roots grow down. In space there is no up and down. These plant parts, unguided by gravity, would probably take on more random orientations.

activity 18

Water the potted plant at its base, so the top of the pot remains drier than the bottom. Because roots are hydrotropic, they will follow the moisture gradient down to the bottom of the pot, anchoring the plant deep in the soil. Watering from above reverses this moisture gradient, resulting in shallow root growth.

activity 19

A. A radish seedling without cotyledons has no stored food reserves to support germination, nor the capacity to photosynthesize until its true leaves develop. Its growth would be severely stunted and it might not survive long enough to grow true leaves.
B. A radish plant without leaves couldn't convert sun energy into stored food energy. It would starve to death unless it could grow new leaves before its food reserves ran out.

activity 20

Radish #1 shows little daily height gain. This suggests that it is older, somewhere near the top of the sigma curve of its growth cycle. Radish #2, by contrast, is still growing rapidly through the middle of its sigma curve. This suggests that it must be younger.

Long-Range Objectives

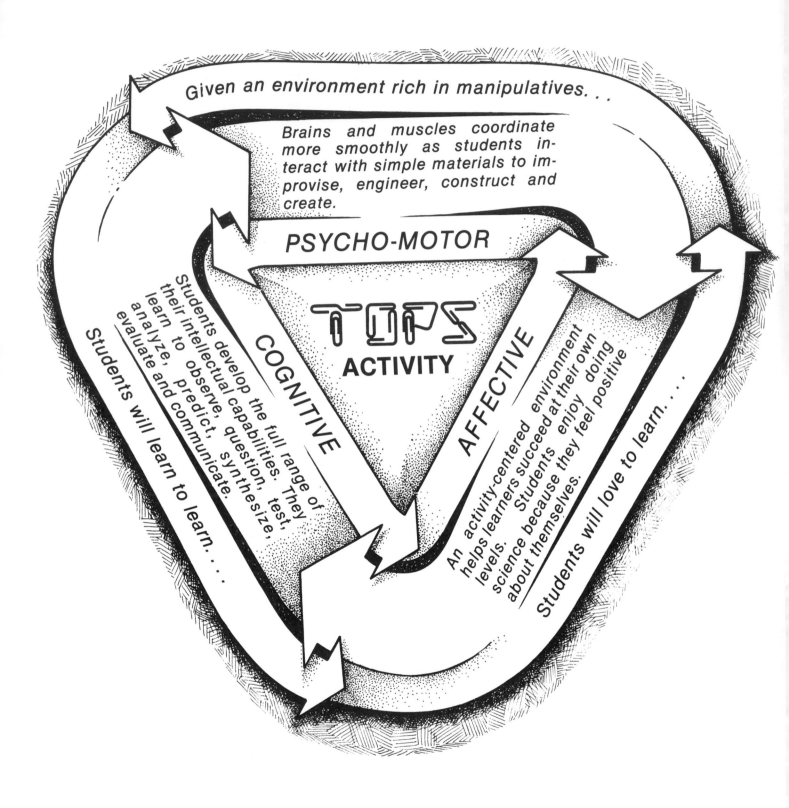

Given an environment rich in manipulatives. . .

Brains and muscles coordinate more smoothly as students interact with simple materials to improvise, engineer, construct and create.

PSYCHO-MOTOR

TOPS ACTIVITY

COGNITIVE

Students develop the full range of their intellectual capabilities. They learn to observe, question, test, analyze, predict, synthesize, evaluate and communicate.

Students will learn to learn. . . .

AFFECTIVE

An activity-centered environment helps learners succeed at their own levels. Students enjoy doing science because they feel positive about themselves.

Students will love to learn. . . .

Gaining A Whole Perspective

Science is an interconnected fabric of ideas woven into broad and harmonious patterns. Use "Extensions" in the teaching notes plus the outline presented below to help your students grasp the big ideas – to appreciate the fabric of science as a unified whole.

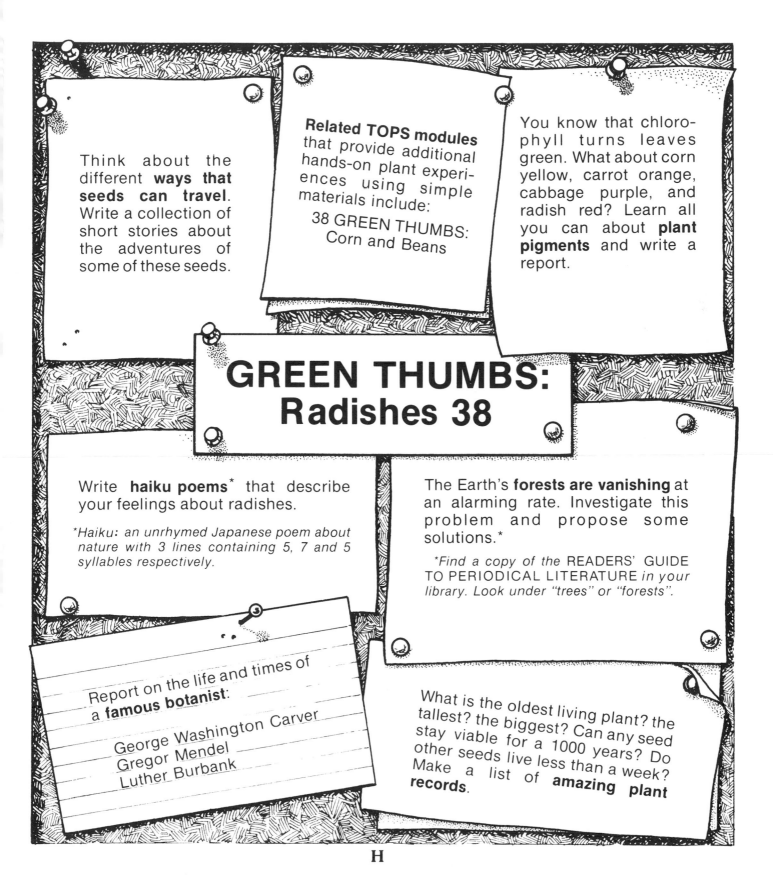

Think about the different **ways that seeds can travel**. Write a collection of short stories about the adventures of some of these seeds.

Related TOPS modules that provide additional hands-on plant experiences using simple materials include:

38 GREEN THUMBS: Corn and Beans

You know that chlorophyll turns leaves green. What about corn yellow, carrot orange, cabbage purple, and radish red? Learn all you can about **plant pigments** and write a report.

GREEN THUMBS: Radishes 38

Write **haiku poems*** that describe your feelings about radishes.

*Haiku: an unrhymed Japanese poem about nature with 3 lines containing 5, 7 and 5 syllables respectively.

The Earth's **forests are vanishing** at an alarming rate. Investigate this problem and propose some solutions.*

*Find a copy of the READERS' GUIDE TO PERIODICAL LITERATURE in your library. Look under "trees" or "forests".

Report on the life and times of a **famous botanist**:

George Washington Carver
Gregor Mendel
Luther Burbank

What is the oldest living plant? the tallest? the biggest? Can any seed stay viable for a 1000 years? Do other seeds live less than a week? Make a list of **amazing plant records**.

ACTIVITIES
AND
LESSON NOTES
1-20

As you distribute these duplicated activity sheets, please observe our copyright notice at the front of this book. We allow you, the purchaser, to make as many copies as you need, but forbid supplying these materials to other teachers or schools.

TOPS is a small, not-for-profit educational corporation, dedicated to making great science accessible to students everywhere. Our only income is from the sale of these inexpensive books. If you would like to help spread the word that TOPS is tops, please request multiple copies of our free TOPS Ideas catalog to pass on to other educators or student teachers. These offer a variety of sample lessons, plus an order form for your colleagues to purchase their own TOPS books. Thanks!

HAPPY BIRTHDAY

1 Close the spout of a clean, dry milk carton with tape. Then snip off the tip of one corner near the spout.

2 Starting in the corner hole, cut along 3 edges as shown. Leave one edge uncut to make a lid with a hinge.

3 Write your name(s) on masking tape. Stick it to the side of your carton.

4 Fold 2 paper towels so they neatly cover the bottom of this *sprout tray*. Turn a smooth layer to the top.

5 Divide this top side into fourths with a ballpoint pen. Draw 5 circles in each quarter, and number them 1-20.

6 Lay the towels in your sprout tray. Soak with water and pour off the excess.

7 Set 1 radish seed in each circle on the towel.

8 Close the lid with masking tape. Fold a small tab at one end so you can open and close the lid easily.

TOPS LEARNING SYSTEMS

Objective

To sprout radish seeds in a warm, moist environment, and organize them for future study.

Lesson Notes

Welcome to Green Thumbs: Radishes, a salad bowl of TOPS activity.

Begin this first lesson by distributing 1 copy of the Master Schedule to every student. Ask them to write their name, and the name of their lab partner (if any) at the top of the paper. Or you might pair lab partners in advance and write in these names yourself.

Locate, with your class, the calendar box at the top of the Monday column in the row designated week 1. This box defines today's assignment. Notice that activities 1 and 2 should be completed to stay on schedule.

Distribute a copy of activities 1 and 2 to each lab group. Students can share these instructions between them, since today they will only be assembling mutual equipment. There are no questions on these pages that require an individual response.

As students finish activity 1 (it takes perhaps 15 minutes), remind them to bring their sprout nurseries to you for evaluation. You will initial your approval in the large box, so they can proceed directly to activity 2.

1-2. Hand strength, good eye-hand coordination, and a sharp pair of heavy duty scissors are all needed to make neat cuts along 3 edges of the milk carton. Assist younger children as necessary.

8. Be sure all lids are shut and remain closed overnight. This will reduce the cooling effects of evaporation and speed seed germination.

Scheduling

Related activities: **1**---3---4---7---9.

Check Point

Are 20 seeds in the sprout nursery, one inside each numbered circle? Are the towels saturated, yet free of excess (standing) water?

Materials

☐ A half-gallon (2 liter) cardboard milk carton.
☐ Scissors. These should be heavy duty, capable of cutting through the coated cardboard of milk cartons. Blunt-nosed children's scissors are not up to the job.
☐ Masking tape.
☐ Paper towels. Purchase a soft, highly-absorbent roll from your local supermarket.
☐ A ballpoint pen.
☐ A source of running water, or a large pitcher or gallon milk jug full of water. This item will be assumed from now on.
☐ 20 radish seeds. Any fast-growing summer variety, maturing in 3-4 weeks, is fine. Champion or Scarlet Globe are suitable. To estimate quantity, assume that each lab group will need 80 seeds altogether, or 1/10 of a seed packet, or enough to plant a 3.5 foot row, or enough to produce a yield of 3 dozen. If you have student helpers, put them to work counting out 80 seeds in envelopes for each lab group. Hand these out with this first activity, and make your students responsible for using and conserving their own radish seeds.
☐ File folders. Even though students work in lab groups, each individual should still be required to complete a full set of activity sheets, then track his or her personal progress on the Master Schedule. These papers are best stored in a folder, Master Schedule on top, and kept on file in class. Students will turn to these folders often to review directions, or to continue work on experiments still in progress.

FOIL MINI-PLANTERS

1 Cut 4 pieces of foil to the size of 4x6 index cards. . .

. . .then fold each piece in half the long way.

2 Stick masking tape around the **positive** end of a battery, even with the edge.

POSITIVE END

TAPE AT EDGE

3 Wrap a foil piece around the battery so the folded side **just meets** the masking tape. . .

EDGE OF TAPE   FOLD

. . . then fold over the ends and push them flat against your table.

FOLD   FLATTEN

4 Tape the top edge of the seam with a **small** piece of tape. Number the tape like this **before** you pull out the battery.

2A

Then make 3 more mini-planters.

2B   2C   2D

5 Fill each mini-planter **brim full** with moist potting soil.

A   2B   2C   2D

DAMP SOIL

6 Poke pencil holes into planters **2A** and **2B**. Make the holes pencil-point deep.

PENCIL-POINT DEEP

2A   2B

Set **2C** and **2D** aside. . .

2C   2D

7 Drop 2 radish seeds into each hole.

2A   2B

USE ONLY THESE 2 PLANTERS FOR NOW

8 Cover the seeds with soil.

2A   2B

9 Get a styrofoam tray and write your name(s) on the side.

MARA + SH

10 Stand all 4 mini-planters inside...

2A   2B   2C   2D

Keep a little water in the bottom.

TOPS LEARNING SYSTEMS

Objective

To construct foil mini-planters for growing radish seeds in potting soil.

Lesson Notes

Make a set of mini-planters in advance and set them in a watering tray to provide a model for your students to emulate. Activity page directions make more sense when students understand the end product that they are working toward. Moreover, in case both radish seeds in any student's planter fail (with fresh seed, the chances are about 1 in 300), you can step in and donate one of your own planters.

2-3. The masking tape serves as a measuring guide, allowing students to construct planters of uniform height. There will be just enough foil overlapping the end to secure a solid bottom.

Younger students may find these foil containers a bit too flimsy. If this is a problem, try substituting heavy duty oven foil. Or provide the ultimate radish planter, a film canister with a hole poked in the bottom. You can reuse these each year. Give your pharmacist or film processor plenty of advance notice to collect the 10 per activity group that your class will ultimately need.

4. Emphasize that only short pieces of tape are needed. Students commonly use excessive amounts.

6-8. Punch holes in the soil to their proper pencil-point depth. If the seeds remain too near the surface, the roots will not penetrate deeply enough to properly support the developing seedlings. If the seed are planted excessively deep, they will take too long to sprout.

10. Overzealous young farmers tend to drown their young charges in water. This deprives the roots of oxygen and promotes rot. But if your styrofoam trays are shallow, as recommended, the sprouts are guaranteed adequate drainage.

Absentminded farmers might forget to make a scheduled watering. As long as they flood the tray before the soil dries out completely, the seedlings should survive. Roots will grow deeper, seeking moisture at the bottom of the planter, thereby firmly establishing each sprout. Even in very dry climates, one good watering on Friday should always carry all the radishes into a moist Monday.

Scheduling

Related activities: **2**---7---10---12---14---19.

It's OK to finish this activity a day late.

Check Point

Are all four planters properly labeled? Are student names on the watering tray? Does everyone understand the importance of occasionally flooding the bottom of the tray with water?

Materials

☐ Aluminum foil. Purchase 12-inch rolls if available; two 4x6 inch index cards placed end to end fit perfectly across this width. If younger students can't tear even pieces off the roll, pre-tear a single 8x12 inch sheet of foil for each lab group, for students to subdivide into 4 pieces. (See note 2-3.)

☐ A 4x6 inch index card.

☐ Scissors. Light duty are OK for all remaining activities.

☐ Masking tape, 3/4 inch wide.

☐ A size-D battery, dead or alive. Make sure it is not leaking.

☐ Transparent tape with matte surface that accepts writing. Or use masking tape.

☐ Moist potting soil. Purchase a small bag of house plant mix in any variety store that features a garden center. Premix perhaps a quart of this soil in a bowl with water until thoroughly moist. You can also cut a corner from the bag, add water a little at a time, and knead until evenly moist. (Digging your own soil risks importing extraneous weeds, molds and fungi into your classroom. Commercial potting mixes are sterilized, and assure good drainage.)

☐ 4 radish seeds.

☐ A styrofoam tray measuring about 6x8 inches (equivalent in area to half a sheet of paper) and no more than 1 inch deep. Meat trays often have these dimensions. Lids cut from styrofoam egg cartons also work well. The tray must be large enough to accommodate up to 10 foil mini-planters at one time.

SPROUT DRAWINGS

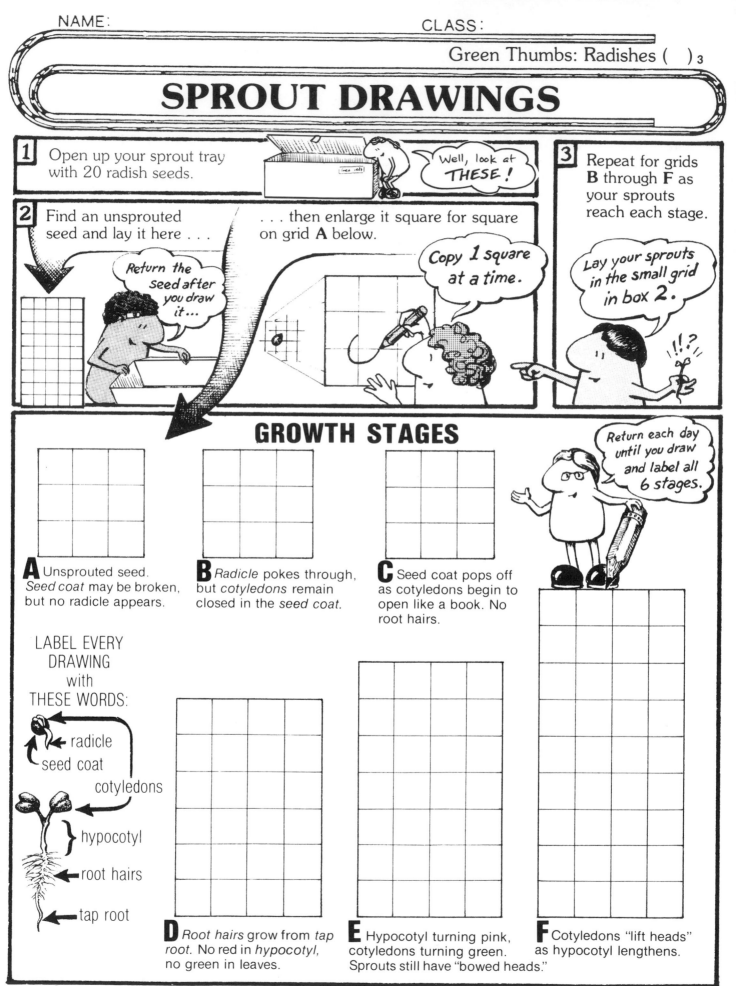

1 Open up your sprout tray with 20 radish seeds.

Well, look at THESE !

2 Find an unsprouted seed and lay it here . . .

. . . then enlarge it square for square on grid **A** below.

Return the seed after you draw it . . .

Copy 1 square at a time.

3 Repeat for grids **B** through **F** as your sprouts reach each stage.

Lay your sprouts in the small grid in box 2.

GROWTH STAGES

Return each day until you draw and label all 6 stages.

A Unsprouted seed. *Seed coat* may be broken, but no radicle appears.

B *Radicle* pokes through, but *cotyledons* remain closed in the *seed coat*.

C Seed coat pops off as cotyledons begin to open like a book. No root hairs.

LABEL EVERY
DRAWING
with
THESE WORDS:

← radicle
seed coat
cotyledons
← hypocotyl
← root hairs
← tap root

D *Root hairs* grow from *tap root*. No red in *hypocotyl*, no green in leaves.

E Hypocotyl turning pink, cotyledons turning green. Sprouts still have "bowed heads."

F Cotyledons "lift heads" as hypocotyl lengthens.

TOPS LEARNING SYSTEMS

Objective

To observe how seedlings develop and grow. To record small details and overall proportions with the aid of a drawing grid.

Lesson Notes

1. It is now Tuesday. Twenty-four hours have passed since you first exposed the radish seeds to moisture. If overnight temperatures inside the sprout nursery have been moderate, perhaps half the seeds will have sprouted. You may find more sprouts if the temperature was warmer, fewer if cooler.

2-3. Some students may find entry into this activity a bit difficult. Explain that their task is twofold. First, find a seedling in the sprout nursery (that has reached a defined growth stage) to lay on the small grid in box 2. Second, draw the seedling (on the appropriate larger grid) so it matches the real object square for square. (Don't forget to return the live specimen to its numbered position inside the sprout nursery.)

Only one seedling needs to be drawn for each of the six growth stages. Any unsprouted seed will work in grid A. Any sprouted seed with seed coat attached is appropriate for grid B, etc. Not all stages, of course, will be drawn on the first day. Students typically identify stages A, B and C on Tuesday, stage D on Wednesday and stages E and F on Thursday.

Because this experiment is in progress over 3 days, it has smaller check boxes on the Master Schedule for Tuesday and Wednesday. Students should check off these boxes themselves to signify completion of each day's work. You check the entire activity sheet on Thursday, initialing your final approval in the larger box.

Remind students to handle their seedlings gently. Radishes are tough, as young seedlings go, but they can still be injured by insensitive fingers.

A-F. Ask students to take all the time they need to produce accurate drawings, to capture and enlarge as much detail as possible. (One-half hour is not too long to spend. BAR GRAPHS, the second experiment for today, requires only about 10 minutes of work.)

A sharp pencil and good eraser are essential to hone and refine each drawing. You might illustrate the difference between a careful drawing and a careless one on your blackboard. If you make accurate drawings a big issue, students will reward you and themselves with excellent work.

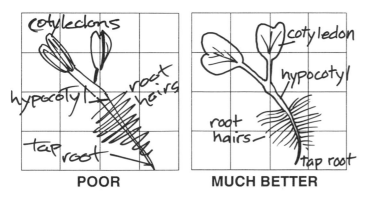

POOR   **MUCH BETTER**

The names of some parts of the seedling will be unfamiliar to your students. List this vocabulary along with phonetic pronunciations on your blackboard. Then review each word aloud with your class:

>   cotyledon (cot-uh-LEE-dun)
>   hypocotyl (HY-poe-cot-uhl)
>   radicle (RA-duh-cul)

On Wednesday, ask your class to check that their paper towels are still thoroughly moist. If your climate is dry, or sprout nursery lids have been left open, additional water may be needed.

Scheduling

Related activities: 1---**3**---4.

Model Answers

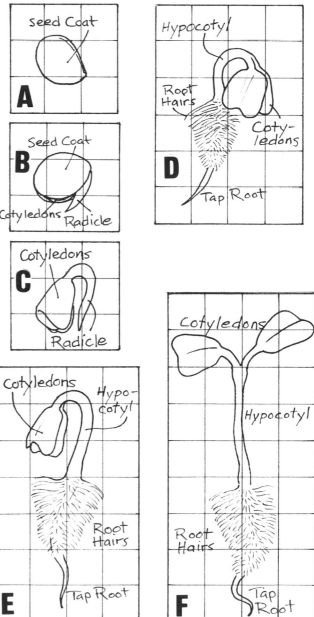

Materials

☐ The milk carton sprout nursery from activity 1.
☐ A sharp pencil and soft, clean eraser.

BAR GRAPHS

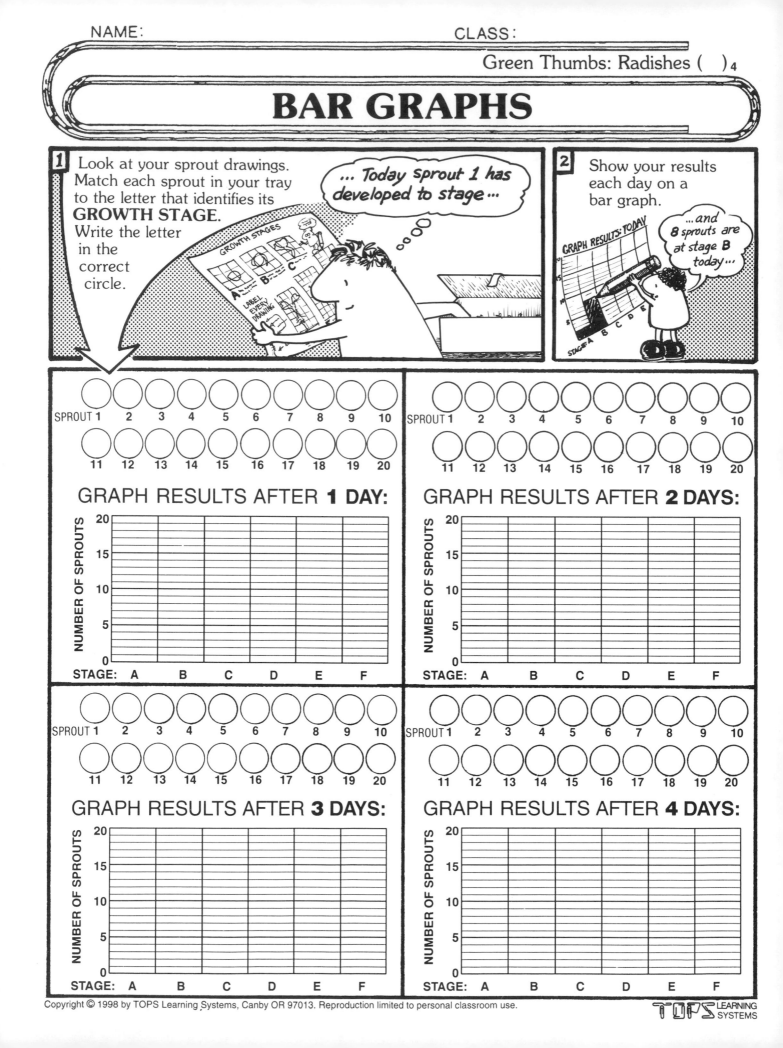

Objective

To classify stages of development in 20 radish seedlings. To visually express daily development profiles on a bar graph.

Lesson Notes

As your Master Schedule indicates, begin this lesson on Tuesday, right after completing all possible SPROUT DRAWINGS. Return each day, Tuesday through Friday, to complete another bar graph.

1. This step is twofold. First match each radish, 1-20, to a Growth Stage drawing that describes its current development, then record the letter associated with this stage in each corresponding circle above the bar graph being completed.

Occasionally a strong seed coat may bind the cotyledons together longer than normal. If this happens, root hairs might appear (stage D) before the seed coat pops off (stage C). Any seedling in this condition should be classified as having reached D stage development.

Root hairs are so thin and numerous that, taken together, they look somewhat like furry white mold. Their development dramatically increases the root's surface area, and thus its ability to absorb water.

As the hypocotyl lengthens (stage F), it may temporarily lose its radish-red flush of color (stage E). This color will return later as the plant matures. (Some radish varieties or individual sprouts may not show this initial flash of color at all.)

Notice that 20 blocks have been filled in for each graph under Model Answers. These represent 4 daily snapshots in time that document the development of 20 radish seeds. No single radish seed was ever recorded as having passed through all 6 stages. There are, after all, only 4 graphs. Many stages for individual sprouts were simply unobserved and unrecorded between snapshots. Nor did every seedling pass through all 6 stages. Some with especially strong seed coats may have skipped stage C. Others lacking pink in their hypocotyls did not pass through stage E.

Scheduling

Related activities: 1---3---**4**---8.

You can start activity 5 a day early, but don't go beyond step 6 (don't add seeds yet).

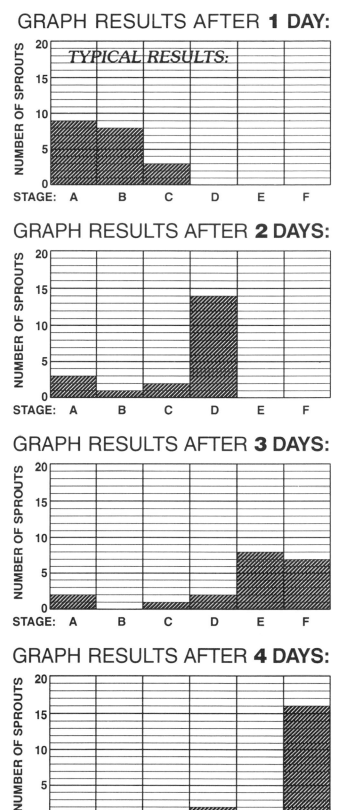

Model Answers

GRAPH RESULTS AFTER **1 DAY:**

GRAPH RESULTS AFTER **2 DAYS:**

GRAPH RESULTS AFTER **3 DAYS:**

GRAPH RESULTS AFTER **4 DAYS:**

Materials

☐ Milk carton sprout nursery.
☐ Sprout drawings from activity 3.

FOUR ENVIRONMENTS

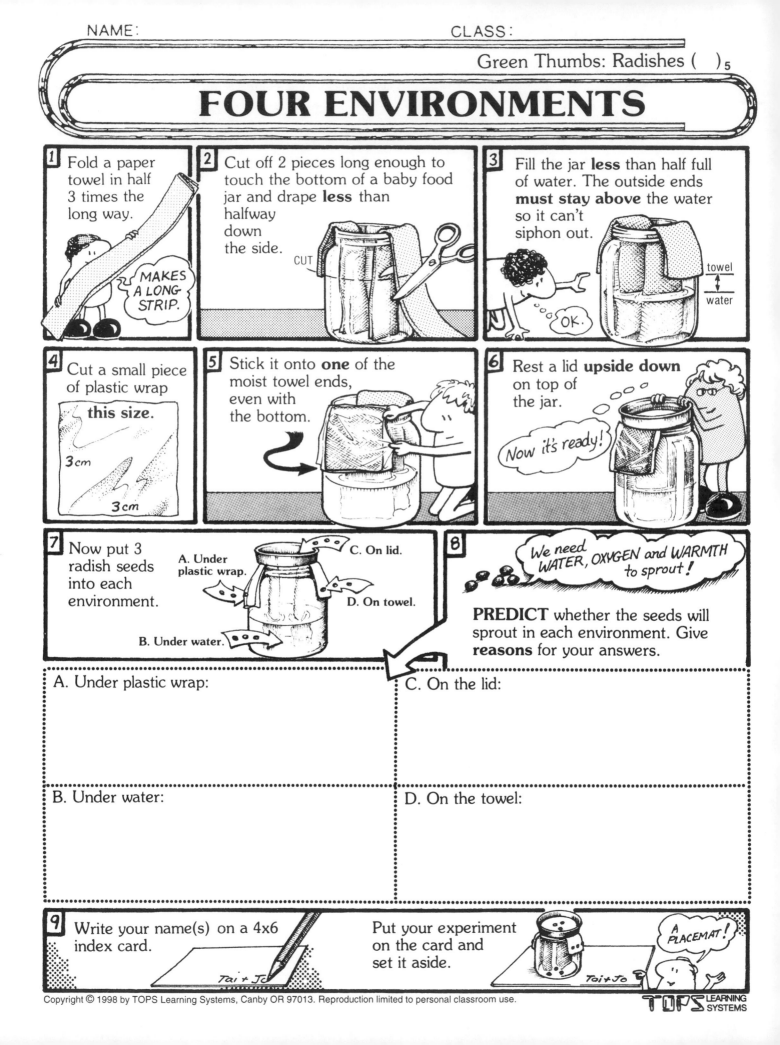

1 Fold a paper towel in half 3 times the long way.

MAKES A LONG STRIP.

2 Cut off 2 pieces long enough to touch the bottom of a baby food jar and drape **less** than halfway down the side.

CUT

3 Fill the jar **less** than half full of water. The outside ends **must stay above** the water so it can't siphon out.

OK.

towel
water

4 Cut a small piece of plastic wrap **this size.**

3 cm
3 cm

5 Stick it onto **one** of the moist towel ends, even with the bottom.

6 Rest a lid **upside down** on top of the jar.

Now it's ready!

7 Now put 3 radish seeds into each environment.

A. Under plastic wrap.
C. On lid.
D. On towel.
B. Under water.

8 We need WATER, OXYGEN and WARMTH to sprout!

PREDICT whether the seeds will sprout in each environment. Give **reasons** for your answers.

A. Under plastic wrap:

C. On the lid:

B. Under water:

D. On the towel:

9 Write your name(s) on a 4x6 index card.

Tai + Jo

Put your experiment on the card and set it aside.

A PLACEMAT!

Tai + Jo

TOPS LEARNING SYSTEMS

Objective

To sprout radish seeds in 4 unique environments, controlling all important variables.

Lesson Notes

2-3. Beware the siphon effect. If the towel hanging over the outside of the jar extends below the water level inside, then water will continue to flow through the towel and trickle down the outside of the jar until the water level is level with the end of the overhanging towel.

5. This small plastic patch rests even with, not below, the end of the towel. If the plastic hangs lower than the water level inside, it too will siphon water out of the jar.

7-8. To prepare your students to make thoughtful predictions, they need to understand the characteristics of all 4 environments in terms of water, free oxygen and temperature. Discuss which environments have more and which have less. Summarize your conclusions on the blackboard by ranking the environments along a relative scale.

WATER: Water is obviously most abundant in the jar (B). The seeds on the wet towel covered with plastic (A) are surrounded by more moisture than the uncovered ones (D). Water is pretty scarce in the dry lid (C).

OXYGEN: Seeds need at least some free oxygen (gaseous O_2) in order to respire — get energy for sprouting and growing. This oxygen is much more abundant in air than in water. Water does contain some dissolved oxygen, however. Ask any fish.

TEMPERATURE: The jar of water and its lid assume the same temperature as the ambient air in your classroom. The seeds on the lid and those under water must therefore be near room temperature.

But the seeds exposed on the moist towel are cooler than room temperature, because water continually evaporates off the towel, carrying heat away in the process. This is easy to demonstrate. Ask students to dip one finger in water, and keep another finger dry. Then wave both fingers in the air. The wet finger feels noticeably cooler.

The seeds under the plastic wrap, by contrast, can be warmer than room temperature. When light passes through plastic, some of its energy is trapped underneath as heat: the greenhouse effect. Further, this warming is not overcome by the cooling effects of evaporation, because the plastic barrier prevents water molecules from escaping into the air.

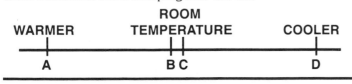

Don't tell your class which groups of seeds will sprout. Limit your discussion to a comparison of variables in the 4 environments. Let your students do their own predicting. Many will predict wrong, but this is the nature of discovery science.

9. These index card "placemats" serve to identify the owners of experiments in progress that are not otherwise labeled. Each lab group should store this next to their sprout tray.

Your students will examine their seeds 8 days from now and evaluate how well they predicted. In the meantime, water keeps evaporating from the exposed towel and slowly drains the jar. Check the level from time to time and refill halfway as necessary.

Scheduling

Related activities: **5---9---13**.

It's OK to finish this activity a day late. You can also start activity 6 a day early, but don't go beyond step 6.

Extension

Investigate how cold temperatures influence radish seeds. Try to sprout some seeds in a refrigerator on a moist paper towel. (They won't sprout.)

Model Answers

8A. The seeds will sprout. They have moisture and some exposure to oxygen in air. The plastic warms them by the greenhouse effect and prevents cooling by evaporation.

8B. The seeds might sprout. They have water, and are near room temperature. But they have little free oxygen under water.

8C. The seeds will not sprout. The lid is too dry.

8D. The seeds will not sprout. Rapid evaporation from the surface of the wet towel keeps them too cold.

Materials

☐ A paper towel.
☐ Scissors.
☐ A baby food jar and lid.
☐ Plastic wrap.
☐ 12 radish seeds.
☐ A 4x6 index card.

NIGHT AND DAY

1 Tear off a piece of aluminum foil about 12 cm long.

| 1 | 2 | 3 | 4 | 5 | 6 | 7 | 8 | 9 | 10 | 11 | 12 cm |

2 Roll up a baby food jar so the foil sticks out past both ends— more at the bottom and less at the top.

LESS
MORE

3 Fold the foil over so **no light** can pass through the glass.

Crimp foil around rim.

Fold under and press flat.

4 Fold a paper towel in half 3 times to make a small rectangle.

5 Draw 2 circles on this folded towel by tracing around the mouth of a baby food jar.

6 Cut out both circles.
Put one stack in the foil jar, and the other in a clear jar.

LAY THEM IN NEATLY.

7 Soak the towel circles with a little water, then pour out the excess.

SOAK   DRAIN

8 Put 4 radish seeds on the wet towels in each jar. Press the lids on tightly and tape over the tops.

1, 2, 3, 4

9 Will these seeds sprout and grow? Give reasons for each prediction.

FOIL JAR:

CLEAR JAR:

10 Put both jars on your index card place mat with activity 5.

Tai + Jo

TOPS LEARNING SYSTEMS

Objective

To study the effects of light and darkness on the germination and growth of radish seeds.

Lesson Notes

1. Measure the aluminum against the ruler provided. Using a foot-wide roll of foil, you should end up with a piece that measures roughly 12 cm by 30 cm.

2-3. Notice that the jar is rolled up along the length of this foil. This will completely cover the sides. The 12 cm width provides enough overlap to totally seal the bottom and the rim from all light.

YES   **NO**

6-8. Each paper towel stack contains 8 circles. This much paper easily absorbs enough water to moisturize the sprouting seeds in their sealed environments.

The tape does not seal the jars, it deters curious students from peeking into them prematurely. The foil-covered jar tends to provoke healthy curiosity. But youngsters who yield to temptation will admit unwanted light into the jar, altering the results of the experiment.

9. Most children know that plants need light to grow. It's no surprise, therefore, if students predict that the seeds in the clear jar will sprout, and that ones in the covered jar will not. Those who think a little deeper, about seeds sprouting underground in dark, damp soil, may predict the opposite.

Rightness or wrongness is not the issue here. Good science is. A well-reasoned prediction that is wrong is better than a lucky guess. Six days from now, in activity 11, your students will continue the good science they've started here. They will examine the seeds in both jars and reevaluate their predictions based on this new experimental evidence.

Scheduling

Related activities: **6**---9---11---13.

It's OK to finish this activity a day late.

Check Point

Is the lid on the foil-covered jar taped well enough to discourage premature peeking? Is it thoroughly wrapped so that no outside light can enter? Is the clear jar exposed to reasonably good light, providing good contrast between "day" and "night"? Are both lids closed tightly to lock in moisture?

Model Answers

9. FOIL JAR: The seeds should spout. They're in a dark, somewhat warm, moist environment similar to being underground. The plants will eventually need light to photosynthesize.

CLEAR JAR: The seeds should sprout. They are moist and even warmer, due to the greenhouse effect. Light will enable the seedlings to turn green and photosynthesize.

Materials

☐ A roll of aluminum foil.
☐ 2 baby food jars and lids.
☐ A paper towel.
☐ Scissors.
☐ 8 radish seeds.
☐ Tape.

LIVING SPACE

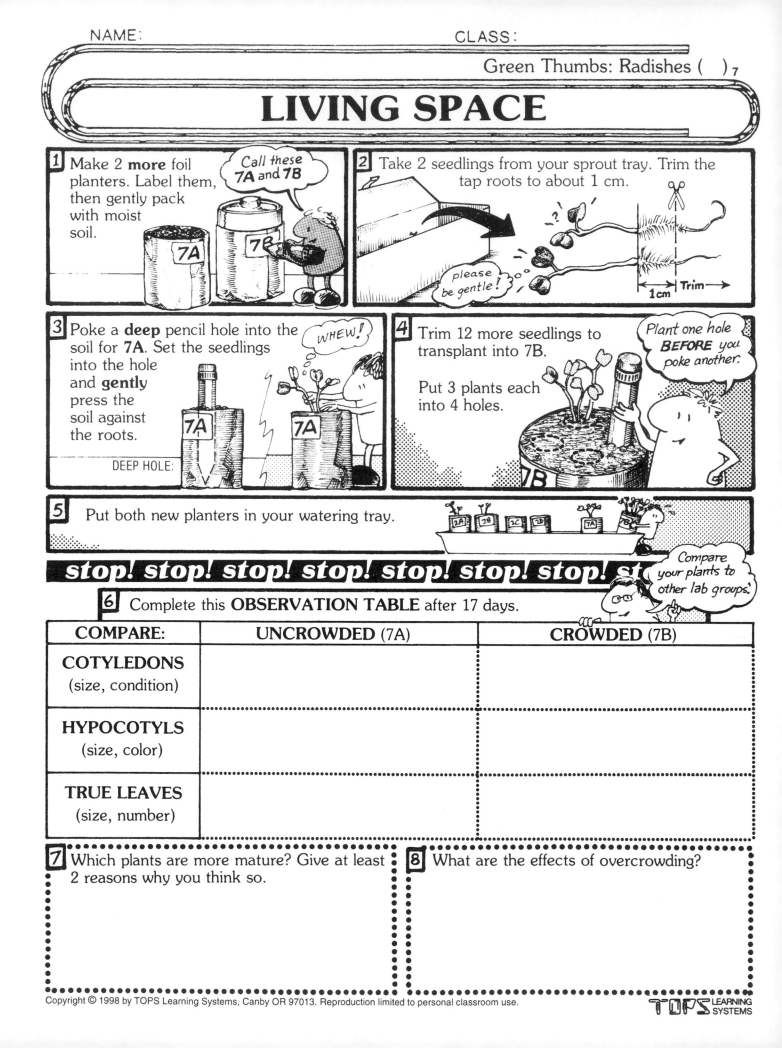

1 Make 2 **more** foil planters. Label them, then gently pack with moist soil. *Call these* **7A** *and* **7B**

2 Take 2 seedlings from your sprout tray. Trim the tap roots to about 1 cm. *please be gentle!* 1cm →Trim→

3 Poke a **deep** pencil hole into the soil for **7A**. Set the seedlings into the hole and **gently** press the soil against the roots. *WHEW!* DEEP HOLE:

4 Trim 12 more seedlings to transplant into 7B. Put 3 plants each into 4 holes. *Plant one hole BEFORE you poke another.*

5 Put both new planters in your watering tray.

stop! stop! stop! stop! stop! stop! stop! st

Compare your plants to other lab groups.

6 Complete this **OBSERVATION TABLE** after 17 days.

COMPARE:	UNCROWDED (7A)	CROWDED (7B)
COTYLEDONS (size, condition)		
HYPOCOTYLS (size, color)		
TRUE LEAVES (size, number)		

7 Which plants are more mature? Give at least 2 reasons why you think so.

8 What are the effects of overcrowding?

TOPS LEARNING SYSTEMS

Objective

To examine the effects of crowded and less crowded growing conditions on radish health and rate of maturation.

Lesson Notes

1. Make new planters as shown. Refer students to activity 2 if they need more detailed direction. Planters 2C and 2D are still unplanted, but don't use them at this time. They will be needed later.

2-4. Trimming the roots makes the seedlings easier to transplant into the pencil holes. Cut them all back to the same 1 cm length. Buy giving each seedling an equal start, the comparison between crowded and uncrowded seedlings in step 6 will be more controlled.

It's relatively easy to transplant just 2 seedlings into one foil planter (step 3). Transplanting a full dozen (step 4) requires more finger coordination and considerable patience. Be ready to assist those who have trouble, so they don't maul their radish seedlings too badly, or stress them beyond their limit of endurance. In general, these techniques are helpful:

- Push groups of 3 seedlings all into one hole at the same time.

- Punch and fill one hole before you poke another.

5. Fourteen radish plants have been transplanted. This leaves 6 seedlings out of your original 20, less any infertile seeds, still in the tray. Disposing of the unchosen few can present a moral dilemma to sensitive adults and children. What to do?

Those who have not "bonded" to their radish seedlings can simply throw them away with a clear conscience. Unlike styrofoam coffee cups and other garbage, radishes dry to almost nothing and decompose, reintegrating naturally into the cosmic fabric. Others who view their seedlings as "children" will want to transplant them to another place where they can continue to "radish" into their full potential.

Season permitting, you can plant them outside, perhaps in a school flower bed or garden. If good growing conditions last for several months, these liberated outdoor radishes will grow many times larger than their indoor relatives that are restricted by limited light and soil. After several months, outdoor radishes send up impressive flowering stalks several feet high to seed new generations.

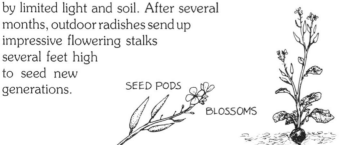

SEED PODS

BLOSSOMS

If the weather is too cold, you can always keep the extra seedlings indoors. Plant them in a large container, with ample growing space: a bucket will do. Fill the bottom third with gravel for good drainage, then the top two thirds with soil from your garden, or planting mix. (You will need more house plant mix for later experiments.) Given enough light and water, these castoffs will grow much larger than their mini-potted neighbors.

After seedlings have been transplanted or discarded, direct students to discard wet towels from the empty sprout tray, and allow the milk carton to dry. If mold is beginning to form, disinfect the cartons with a 10% bleach/90% water solution, or straight hydrogen peroxide (less toxic). These cartons will be recycled in activity 9 as greenhouses.

6-8. Because of genetic differences among seeds, it is possible that robust seedlings in the crowded group will outperform the least vigorous seedlings in the uncrowded group. If you encourage students to compare their results with other lab groups, they should find this to be the exception rather than the rule. Uncrowded radishes do, as a group, grow larger and mature faster than those competing in a crowd.

Under some circumstances, true leaves can be slow to appear. Radishes, a cool-weather crop, can become stressed or even dried out by too much heat in sunny windows or near radiators. Soil must remain moist. Since all green parts of the plant produce nourishment for growth in the presence of light (see notes 11), short winter days limit this capacity. If plants become pale, leggy, and stretch toward the light source, placing them a few inches below an electric lamp overnight can give them the light they're craving.

If after 17 days you don't observe notable gains in the uncrowded group (deep redness and enlargement of the hypocotyl, greater development of true leaves, a pronounced withering of the seed leaves), postpone these steps perhaps a week longer. As an extension, track differences over several months.

Scheduling

Related Activities: 1---2---**7**.

Model Answers

6. **Uncrowded Cotyledons:** These are larger, beginning to turn yellow. (Yellowing or shrivelling of cotyledons is not a sign of poor health, but occurs naturally as seedlings consume food reserves stored in these structures. See Background under Teaching Notes 19.)

Crowded Cotyledons: Smaller, still green.

Uncrowded Hypocotyls: These are fatter, turning reddish.

Crowded Hypocotyls: Thinner, still light green.

Uncrowded True Leaves: These are larger, with second pairs emerging.

Crowded True Leaves: Smaller, with only one pair so far.

7. The uncrowded plants are more mature. Their cotyledons are larger, yellowing; hypocotyls are fatter, redder; and they have more and larger pairs of true leaves.

8. Overcrowded radishes grow smaller and mature less rapidly. They don't look as healthy as the less crowded radishes.

Materials

- ☐ Aluminum Foil.
- ☐ A 4x6 index card.
- ☐ Scissors.
- ☐ Radish seedlings from the sprout tray of activity 1.
- ☐ A size-D battery.
- ☐ Tape.
- ☐ Moist potting soil.

SPROUT GRAPH

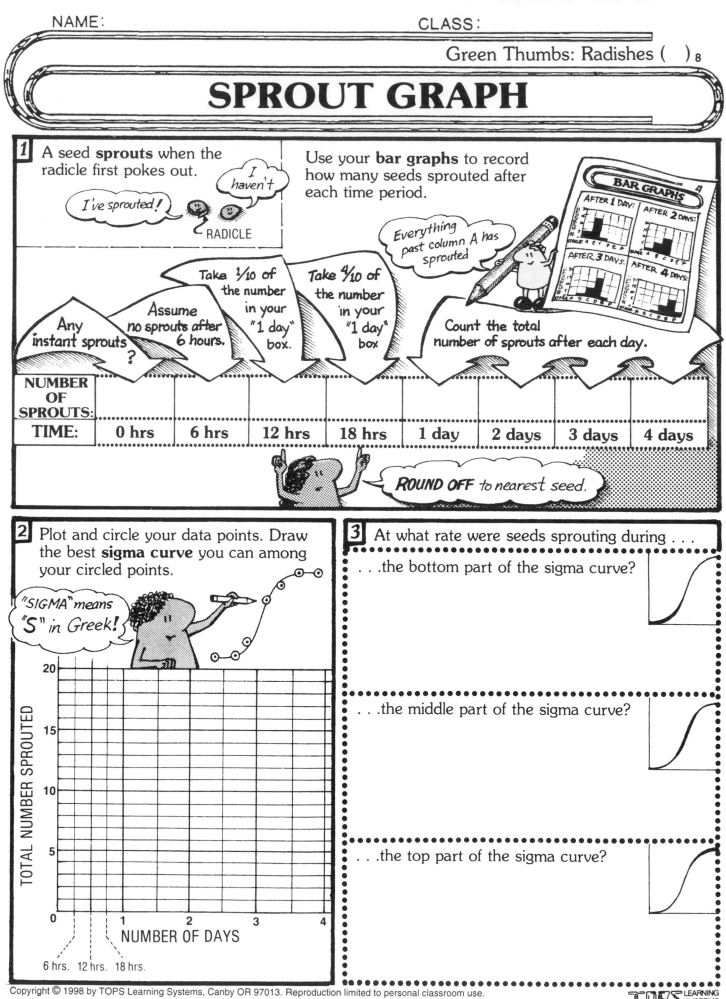

1 A seed **sprouts** when the radicle first pokes out.

I've sprouted!

I haven't

RADICLE

Use your **bar graphs** to record how many seeds sprouted after each time period.

BAR GRAPHS

AFTER 1 DAY: AFTER 2 DAYS:

AFTER 3 DAYS: AFTER 4 DAYS:

Everything past column A has sprouted

Any instant sprouts?

Assume no sprouts after 6 hours.

Take 1/10 of the number in your "1 day" box.

Take 4/10 of the number in your "1 day" box

Count the total number of sprouts after each day.

NUMBER OF SPROUTS:								
TIME:	0 hrs	6 hrs	12 hrs	18 hrs	1 day	2 days	3 days	4 days

ROUND OFF to nearest seed.

2 Plot and circle your data points. Draw the best **sigma curve** you can among your circled points.

"SIGMA" means "S" in Greek!

TOTAL NUMBER SPROUTED

20

15

10

5

0   1   2   3   4
NUMBER OF DAYS

6 hrs. 12 hrs. 18 hrs.

3 At what rate were seeds sprouting during . . .

. . .the bottom part of the sigma curve?

. . .the middle part of the sigma curve?

. . .the top part of the sigma curve?

TOPS LEARNING SYSTEMS

Objective

To plot sprouting rate in a population of radish seeds on a graph. To interpret a sigma curve.

Lesson Notes

Radish seeds, like students, are individuals. Some start fast. Most are average. A few start slow, if at all. Continuums of this nature generate a classic S-shape, sometimes called a sigma curve or sigmoid.

In this activity, your class will take last week's sprouting statistics displayed on daily bar graphs (activity 4) and generate a new composite graph.

1. You can't look in on sprouting radish seeds only once a day and expect to collect enough data to generate a good sigma curve. By the time you take your first look, much of the sprouting action will already be over. Ideally, you should observe the seeds hourly over a period of several days.

Staying up around the clock, we found that radishes generally don't sprout during the first six hours. Typically, 10% of the ones that sprouted by the end of the first day did so after only 12 hours, and another 40% of these sprouted by 18 hours. We incorporated our findings into this step so your class won't have to keep watch all night to generate good graphs.

2. Beginning science students approach data points as if they were working a connect-the-dot puzzle. The end result often looks more like an economic indicator than a smooth curve. You can demonstrate how to draw the best smooth curve through scattered points as follows:

First draw graph coordinates on your blackboard, then plot a typical array of points. While your students watch, surround each point with a circle. Explain that these circles are meant to protect the hard data points they enclose, keeping them from being obscured by the arbitrary graph line you will draw next.

Now sketch the best smooth curve you can to capture the overall trend of these data points. Most points should fall on or near the line, but they don't all need to land dead center. Stop your line at the perimeter of circles you encounter, continuing again at the other side, leaving the points inside unobscured.

3. Only a few seeds sprout initially. They lead an avalanche of many seeds sprouting at nearly the same time, followed by an occasional sprouting laggard.

Students often confuse this sprouting pattern with growing. They typically write that their radishes first grew slow, then fast, then slow again. While radish growth rates do model a sigma curve (see activity 20), *sprouting time* is the variable now under consideration.

Discussion

Sprouting seeds are analogous to popping corn. Why not have a party to illustrate the similarity between sprouts and pops? Bring an electric popper into your classroom, add popcorn and plug it in. While the popper warms up, draw a large version of this graph on your blackboard.

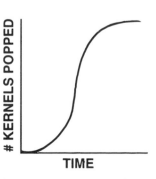

Point to the beginning of the S-curve with the end of a meter stick. Move through the curve as the first few tentative pops evolve into a noisy roar, then subside again to an occasional pop.

If all of this sounds like too much trouble, just skip the popcorn and use your imagination. Add your own sound effects as you trace the graph line. You can repeat the exercise with your class providing a chorus of finger-snaps.

Scheduling

Related Activities: 1---3---4---**8**.

It's OK to finish this activity a day or two late. You can start activity 9 a day early, but don't go beyond step 10.

Model Answers

1.

# Sprouts:	0	0	1	4	11	16	17	18
Time:	0 hrs	6 hrs	12 hrs	18 hrs.	1 day	2 day	3 day	4 day

2.

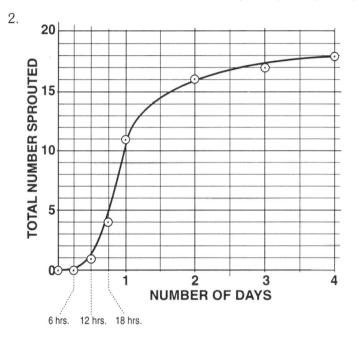

3. During the bottom part of the curve, the sprouting rate was slow (only 1 sprout from 0 to 12 hours);

During the middle part of the curve, the sprouting rate hit a maximum (12 to 24 hours);

During the top part of the curve the sprouting rate got slower and slower (only 2 sprouts during the last 2 days).

Materials

☐ Bar graph results from activity 4.

BUILD A GREENHOUSE

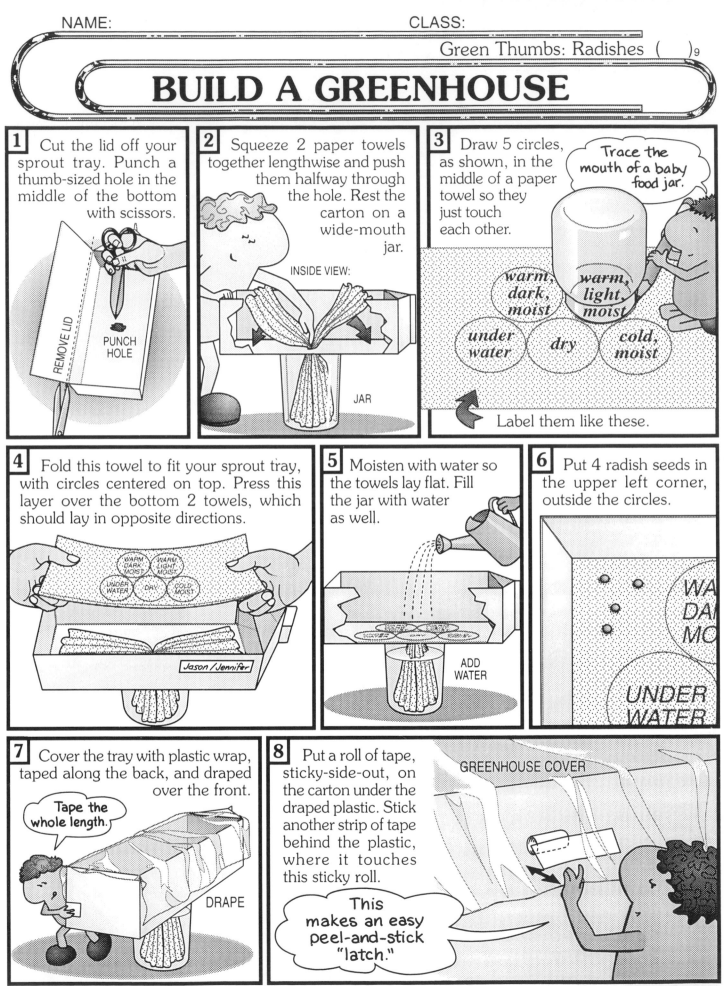

1 Cut the lid off your sprout tray. Punch a thumb-sized hole in the middle of the bottom with scissors.

REMOVE LID   PUNCH HOLE

2 Squeeze 2 paper towels together lengthwise and push them halfway through the hole. Rest the carton on a wide-mouth jar.

INSIDE VIEW:

JAR

3 Draw 5 circles, as shown, in the middle of a paper towel so they just touch each other.

Trace the mouth of a baby food jar.

warm, dark, moist   warm, light, moist

under water   dry   cold, moist

Label them like these.

4 Fold this towel to fit your sprout tray, with circles centered on top. Press this layer over the bottom 2 towels, which should lay in opposite directions.

WARM DARK MOIST   WARM LIGHT MOIST

UNDER WATER   DRY   COLD MOIST

Jason / Jennifer

5 Moisten with water so the towels lay flat. Fill the jar with water as well.

ADD WATER

6 Put 4 radish seeds in the upper left corner, outside the circles.

WA DA MO

UNDER WATER

7 Cover the tray with plastic wrap, taped along the back, and draped over the front.

Tape the whole length.

DRAPE

8 Put a roll of tape, sticky-side-out, on the carton under the draped plastic. Stick another strip of tape behind the plastic, where it touches this sticky roll.

GREENHOUSE COVER

This makes an easy peel-and-stick "latch."

TOPS LEARNING SYSTEMS

Objective

To construct a self-watering greenhouse environment for maintaining and observing radish seedlings.

Lesson Notes

3. Labeling the towel in this way prepares the greenhouse for accommodating seedlings from activities 5 and 6. Keep the circles close together so all 5 fit on the floor of the milk carton.

5. Water will naturally wick up from the jar underneath, keeping the seedlings continually moist. Add liquid plant food to this water (optional) to grow healthier radishes.

6. The seeds you put here will germinate into the young sprouts required for activity 15.

7. A square foot of plastic wrap (30 cm by 30 cm) is sufficient. The seedlings will not generally require "head room" beyond the top of the milk carton.

8. Notice that the sticky roll of masking tape contacts the back of the masking tape strip in this "sticky latch." This makes handling the plastic easier, facilitates opening and closing the latch, and extends its useful life.

Keep the greenhouse closed to help germinate the 4 radish seeds. This minimizes the cooling effects of evaporation, providing a warm, humid growing environment.

As the seedlings grow, however, avoid overheating them in direct sunlight. Open the plastic cover under these conditions, or move the greenhouse to a cooler location. Radishes like light, but prefer room temperatures. If significant condensation forms under the plastic, it is probably too tropical inside.

With water being wicked up from the big reservoir below, the seedlings can survive for weeks at a time virtually unattended. Molds and aging, not dryness, will eventually do them in.

Scheduling

Related Activities:

1---5---6---**9**---11---13---15.

Check Point

Is the greenhouse sufficiently sealed with plastic wrap to ensure a warm moist environment for the 4 radish seeds to sprout inside?

Materials

☐ The empty sprout nursery constructed in activity 1.
☐ Scissors.
☐ 3 paper towels.
☐ A ballpoint pen.
☐ A baby food jar (or lid) to use as a circle template.
☐ A pint or quart size jar with lid.
☐ 4 radish seeds.
☐ Plastic wrap.
☐ Masking tape.

GRID WORK

1 Cut out a drawing grid from the other paper. Tape it to a 4x6 index card.

DRAWING GRID

NAME(S)

2 Bend a paper clip to a right angle.

90°

3 Tape the paper clip behind the grid so it stands up the long way.

STANDS ALMOST STRAIGHT

4 Move planter 2A in front of the grid, and draw it square for square.

*Look straight on. Draw the **same view** each week.*

2A

Development after 1 WEEK:

	2	3	4	5	6	7	
A							A
B							B
C							C
D							D
E							E
F							F
G							G
H							H
I							I
J							J

stop! stop! stop! stop! stop! stop! stop! stop! stop! stop! stop!

Development after 2 WEEKS:

	1	2	3	4	5	6	7	8	
A									A
B									B
C									C
D									D
E									E
F									F
G									G
H									H
I									I
J									J
K									K

Development after 3 WEEKS:

	1	2	3	4	5	6	7	8	
A									A
B									B
C									C
D									D
E									E
F									F
G									G
H									H
I									I
J									J
K									K

TOPS LEARNING SYSTEMS

Objective

To accurately record the growth of radish seedlings over weekly intervals on a drawing grid.

Lesson Notes

1. Students cut their background grids from the reproduced supplementary sheet you provide. (Find this in the back of the book.) Lab groups may or may not require both grids, depending on how well they work together. See the last 3 paragraphs in teaching note 4 below.

4. Put the vertical grid directly behind the radish seedlings, close enough to touch some of the leaves. Turn the plants so their leaves appear mostly in full view rather than on edge. Each week, as students make a new drawing, remind them to turn their radishes to the same orientation as the week before for easy comparisons.

To reinforce vocabulary, ask students to label their weekly radish drawings. Make an enlarged photocopy of this illustration, or sketch one like it on your blackboard, or simply list the words for students to use as a reference:

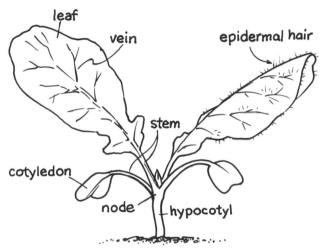

The task is to draw 1 square at a time, transferring what you see framed within each background square to the corresponding (and slightly reduced) activity sheet square. (Letters and numbers at the top and sides correlate squares in both grids.) By dividing the complex radish image into manageable pieces, students can capture overall proportions with greater accuracy.

To minimize distortion, it's important to maintain a straight-on perspective, viewing the radish seedlings directly in front of the background grid. If students are working in pairs, a good deal of cooperation is necessary to avoid bumping heads.

Alternately, you can assign one student to draw planter 2A each week, while the lab partner draws 2B. In this case students will require separate background grids to work simultaneously.

There is only one minor drawback to using both planters. In activity 19, students will snip off a seed leaf and a true leaf from planter 2B for detailed examination. When it comes time to make the final third-week drawing, 2B will be missing two of its leaves. No big deal.

Scheduling

Related Activities: 2---**10**.

Model Answers

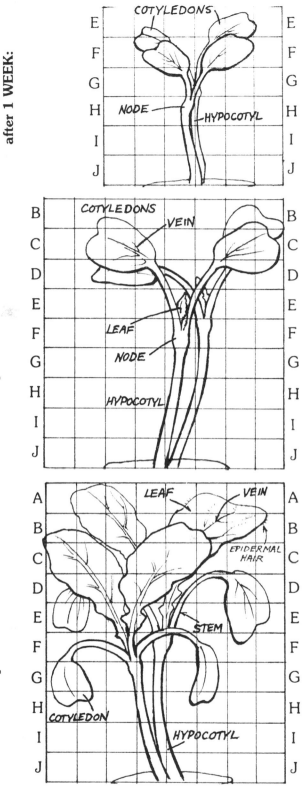

Materials

☐ Supplementary drawing grid. These come two-up on a sheet. Each single grid will serve 1, possibly 2 students.
☐ Scissors.
☐ A paper clip.
☐ A 4x6 inch index card.
☐ Tape.
☐ Radish seedlings from mini-planter 2A (and possibly 2B).

TURN ON THE LIGHTS

1 Get your sealed jars from activity 6.

2 Peel off the tape, pry off the lids, and pull off the foil.

A SURPRISE ?

3 Draw a side view of the seedlings in each jar. Label a **hypocotyl**, **stem** and **cotyledon**.

WITH LIGHT   **WITHOUT LIGHT**

How did the seedlings grow in response to **no** light?

How might this response help the seedling survive?

4 Plants *turn green* when they make **chlorophyll**.

Plants use chlorophyll to *photosynthesize...* turn light energy into food energy *(sugar)*.

GARDEN CLUB

Can radishes make chlorophyll without light? How do you know?

Which parts of the radish are making sugar? How do you know?

5 Look at your sprout predictions in step 9 of activity 6. Did you learn anything new? What?

6 Gently lift the paper circles out of each jar. Put the seedlings into the greenhouse on the correct circles, then reseal the plastic.

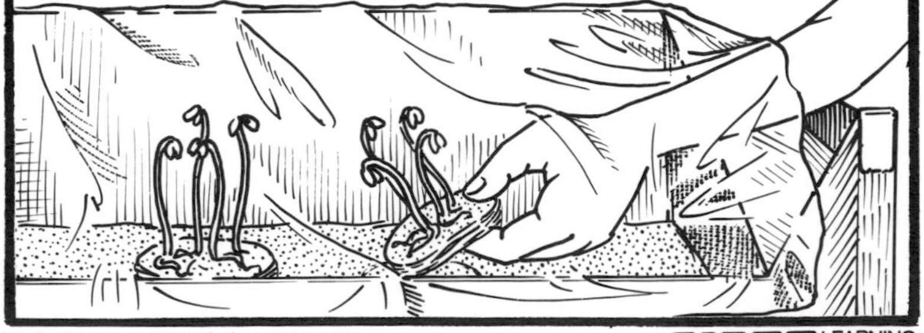

TOPS LEARNING SYSTEMS

Objective

To examine experimental outcomes from activity 6. To understand how lighting conditions affect the growth of radishes and their ability to photosynthesize.

Lesson Notes

2. How will the radish seeds look after 6 days in a moist, dark environment? Will they sprout? Will they grow like the ones in the clear jar? If all foil-covered jars remain sealed with tape, if nobody has peeked, then who can say for sure? Everyone will be curious to find out. It's like opening a present when you don't know what's inside.

You can capitalize on this high interest by engaging your students in a debate before opening the jars. Ask them to share the predictions they made in activity 6, step 9. Where students disagree, encourage them to defend their logic with wonderful reasons. Take a vote on who thinks this and who thinks that. Then open the jars....

4. Once the radish grows into sunlight, it receives the requisite energy for final assembly of its vital chlorophyll molecules. Chlorophyll gives plants their green color. The cotyledons store it in their chloroplasts. Turning dark green, they begin the vital process of photosynthesis. Even the stems help out. Their color changes as well, from white to light green.

Light is essential to plant life. Plants need light energy to photosynthesize — to strip hydrogen from water and combine it with carbon dioxide to produce sugar. Once the food energy stored in the cotyledons is consumed, seedlings must produce additional sugar to fuel their vital functions. No light energy, no chlorophyll, no sugar, no chemical energy, no radish, no life.

6. To get the radishes out of the baby food jar, reach in with your fingers and pull on the towel circles. Don't pull on the seedlings; this will only rip out the roots that have grown into the fibers of the paper towel. Radishes are tough enough to survive some root loss, but they will need several days of recovery in order to develop a new root system.

Scheduling

Related Activities: 6---9---**11**---13.

Model Answers

3.

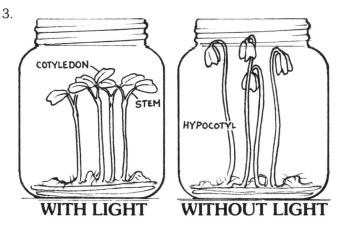

WITH LIGHT   WITHOUT LIGHT

Seedlings with no light: The hypocotyls grew long, thin and colorless. The cotyledons appear yellow with bowed heads.

Survival benefit: Longer seedlings reach higher toward possible light. Bowed heads protect the cotyledons from soil abrasion.

4. Chlorophyll without light? No. Only the light-grown seedlings are colored chlorophyll green. The dark-grown seedlings have no green and therefore no chlorophyll.

Parts making sugar: The cotyledons make the most sugar because they contain the most green chlorophyll. The hypocotyl, colored light green by less chlorophyll, photosynthesizes less sugar.

5. (Answers will vary widely.) Students are typically surprised to see the dark-grown radishes grew so tall.

Materials

☐ Sealed jars from activity 6. One is foil-covered, the other clear.
☐ Greenhouse from activity 9.

PHOTOTROPISM

1 **PHOTOTROPISM** means "turning toward the light."

Photo means LIGHT

Look at your growing radishes. How do you know they are phototropic?

2 Poke a pencil hole into planter **2C**. . .

PENCIL-POINT DEEP

2C

. . . then drop in 4 radish seeds, cover with soil, and moisten the top with water.

2A 2B 2C 2D 7A

stop! stop! stop! stop! stop! stop! stop! stop! stop! stop

return in 6 days:

3 Make a foil "Y." Trace this pattern onto foil and cut it out.

TRACE

CUT

4 Bend a paper clip like this.

Shape the foil around this clip to look like the seedlings in planter 2C.

5 "Plant" your foil seedling in planter **2D**.

2D

6 Put both planters in a lid. Add a little water.

2C 2D

7 Set the lid on your index card where it can rest undisturbed.

2C 2D

8 Now face the sprouts in 2C **away** from the window light.

DAYLIGHT

2C 2D

9 Bend your foil model to predict how 2C will finally grow.

Adjust ALL parts, including the "leaves."

2D

stop! stop! stop!

return in 2 days:

10 Did you correctly predict the final position of the plants in 2C with your foil model? Tell how **cotyledons** and **hypocotyls** respond to light.

TOPS LEARNING SYSTEMS

Objective

To use a radish model to predict how cotyledons and hypocotyls grow to maximize exposure to light.

Lesson Notes

This activity is the first of 3 experiments that explore **tropisms** — how plants respond to external stimuli. Light is studied here; gravity and water tropisms will be considered in activities 17 and 18. If your class is not familiar with the vocabulary of tropisms, introduce it now:

• Define these root words and prefixes on your blackboard:

tropism: turning response	**photo**: light
positive: toward	**geo**: earth
negative: away from	**hydro**: water

• Hook these together into a vocabulary of plant movement Ask volunteers to deduce meanings and give examples of radish parts (if any) that might exhibit such a response.

positive phototropism: turning toward light. *(leaves, stems, hypocotyl)*
positive geotropism: turning toward the earth. *(roots)*
positive hydrotropism: turning toward water. *(roots)*
negative phototropism: turning away from light. *(none)*
negative geotropism: turning away from the earth. *(hypocotyl, stems)*
negative hydrotropism: turning away from water. *(none)*

• Finally, to make tropisms a natural part of each student's vocabulary, try this peppy drill. Designate a water faucet or bucket to represent water; the windows as a symbol of light, the floor as earth. Then define tropisms relative to hand directions. If you say "positive phototropism" for example, students point to the window. Or if you say "negative geotropism," students point up. Speed up the tempo with flashcards. Or simply point and have students chorus back the correct response.

1. Radish seedlings uniformly lean toward the strongest source of sunlight. Turn them away from this source and they tilt back toward it within a day! This only happens, however, if the incoming light is directional, stronger at one angle than everywhere else. If the light in your room is unusually diffuse, you may need to block it on one side (a box will work) so the seedlings will lean away from the shadows you create.

3. Place this "Y" pattern *over* a piece of foil. By tracing with a pencil on this paper pattern, you'll leave an indentation of its image on the foil beneath.

9. As any overdone sunbather knows, skin placed perpendicular to the rays of the sun receives maximum exposure. Radishes "know" this too. By orienting their leaves perpendicular to maximum light, the chlorophyll in their chloroplasts receives the greatest possible energy to photosynthesize.

10. After completing question 10, both planters can be removed from the lid and transferred to the larger watering tray.

Scheduling

Related Activities: **12**---17---18.

After finishing steps 1 and 2 in this activity, it's OK to do the first 2 steps of activity 13 early.

Extension

Place some young, fast-growing radish seedlings near a window so they receive direct sunlight at high noon. (In the northern hemisphere, this will be a window with southern exposure.) Keep them well watered.

Cut a narrow strip along the edge of an index card, stopping about halfway. Bend this "arm" to point to the noon sun so its shadow disappears. After a day or two, compare the angle of this arm with the phototropic growing angle of the seedlings.

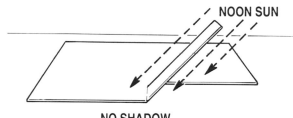

Model Answers

1. The radishes must be phototropic because they all lean in the same direction, toward the source of strongest light.

10. The hypocotyl bends, turning the flat surface of the cotyledons for maximum perpendicular exposure to incoming light rays.

Materials

☐ Watering tray with mini-planters from previous activities.
☐ 4 radish seeds.
☐ Aluminum foil.
☐ Scissors.
☐ A paper clip.
☐ A jar lid. It should be the size of a mayonnaise lid or larger.

GREENHOUSE PREDICTIONS

1 Examine your jar with the 4 different environments.

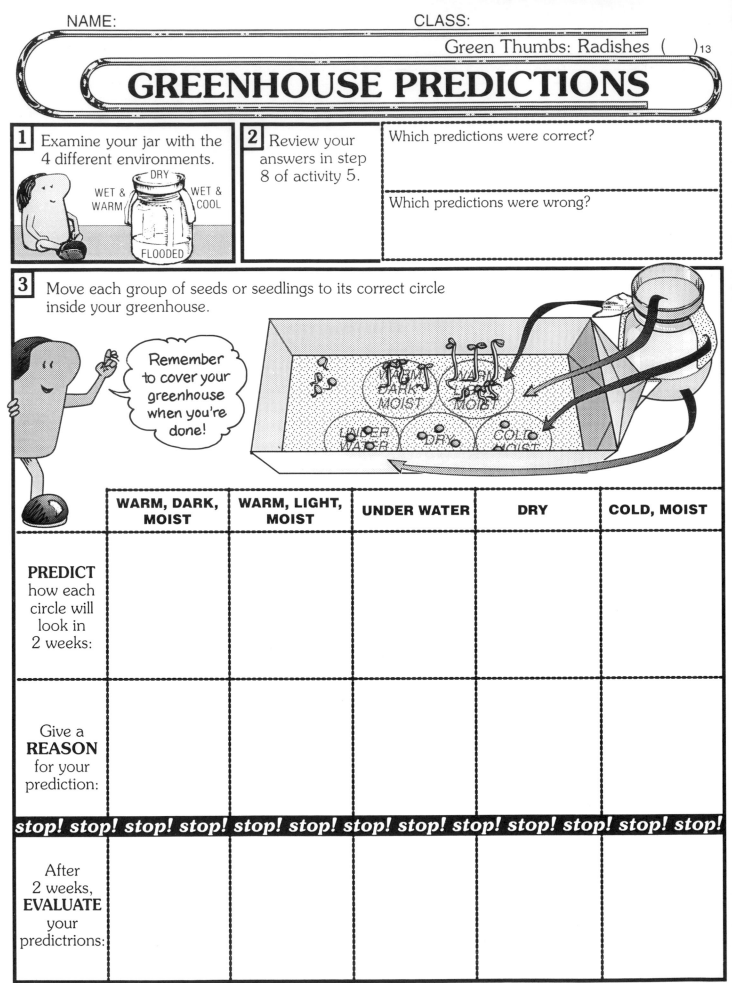

DRY
WET & WARM
WET & COOL
FLOODED

2 Review your answers in step 8 of activity 5.

Which predictions were correct?

Which predictions were wrong?

3 Move each group of seeds or seedlings to its correct circle inside your greenhouse.

Remember to cover your greenhouse when you're done!

WARM, DARK, MOIST
WARM, LIGHT, MOIST
UNDER WATER
DRY
COLD, MOIST

	WARM, DARK, MOIST	WARM, LIGHT, MOIST	UNDER WATER	DRY	COLD, MOIST
PREDICT how each circle will look in 2 weeks:					
Give a **REASON** for your prediction:					
stop! stop! stop! stop! stop! stop! stop! stop! stop! stop! stop! stop! stop!					
After 2 weeks, **EVALUATE** your predictrions:					

TOPS LEARNING SYSTEMS

Objective

To examine experimental outcomes from activity 5. To evaluate previous predictions, then make new ones about how the radishes will continue to grow in their new greenhouse environment.

Lesson Notes

1-2. Allow enough time for students to examine the seeds in each environment and evaluate how accurate their predictions were. Then, before moving on to step 3, summarize all important growth variables studied thus far in a class discussion (see below).

3. The greenhouse already has 3 clusters of radish residents from previous activities. These include 4 young seedlings in the upper left corner, plus radishes in the top two circles. Leave these in place, adding new seeds and seedlings as shown.

Disagreeable molds and mildews will eventually invade your tropical paradise. But your radishes should tolerate this competition and continue to grow normally for the duration of this unit.

Scheduling

Related Activities: 5---6---9---11---**13**.

You can finish the first part of this activity a day late. It's OK to finish the final part a few days late as well.

Discussion

WATER: Absolutely necessary, but not sufficient by itself. Other conditions must also be met.

OXYGEN: Some radish seeds sprouted under water (surprise!), but lacked sufficient oxygen to develop normally. Others didn't germinate at all. Apparently radish seeds require more exposure to oxygen than water can provide.

TEMPERATURE: The radish seeds warmed by the plastic cover successfully germinated. Seeds that were unprotected from cooling by evaporation did not sprout. Moderate or warm temperatures seem necessary.

LIGHT: Radish seeds sprout very well in total darkness. But they need light in order to turn green and photosynthesize.

Will transferring the radish seeds and seedlings to the greenhouse in step 3 now promote normal development for all of them? Not necessarily. Students need to further understand something about a seed's internal metabolism before they can make reasonable predictions.

To focus this part of your discussion, tape a single radish seed to a dry paper towel, then tape the towel to your blackboard for all to see. Ask this question: Do you think this seed is dead or alive right now as you look at it? Accept all opinions that are supported with reasons. Encourage debate.

Introduce the concept of *viability*. A fresh packet of radish seeds might be 95% viable. Put 20 on a moist paper towel and perhaps 19 will sprout. Why? Because 19 are alive and only 1 is dead. Those who argue that the seed taped to your paper towel is alive are most likely correct. There is perhaps a 5% probability that it is dead.

Even though this seed is probably alive right now, its life processes are extremely slow. The tiny embryo inside the seed coat may survive several years in this state of suspended animation. But when its food reserves are finally depleted, it will die. Its only hope of growing into an adult radish is to find itself in a moist, suitable place to grow. The dry paper towel is too much of a desert!

Now moisten the area surrounding the seed with a few drops of water. Giving water to this seed is a clarion call to awaken and grow. Life processes, formerly in slow motion, now shift into high gear. Food reserves that would last years in a dry state will now be consumed in a matter of days. Will this radish seed be able to successfully photosynthesize its own food (sprout and turn green) before its food reserves run out? Yes, if it gets other essentials (air, warmth and light), before its food reserves run so low that development is impaired.

Now pick the radish seed off the towel, remove the tape and plant it in some moist soil. Present this planted seed to your class and ask if it will develop normally. (This one probably will.) Then ask if seeds in each greenhouse circle (some deprived of oxygen and warmth, with metabolisms accelerated by moisture) can do as well. Require thoughtful written predictions in the first 10 boxes of step 3.

Model Answers

2. Answers will vary.

3. Predictions / Reasons:

WARM, DARK, MOIST: They'll turn green and unfold their cotyledons. Light will enable normal chlorophyll production.

WARM, LIGHT, MOIST: They'll continue to grow normally. Previous growing conditions were favorable.

UNDER WATER: They will not sprout at all, or remain severely stunted. They were deprived of oxygen needed to metabolize food.

DRY: They'll sprout and develop normally. Earlier dry conditions preserved their food reserves.

COOL, MOIST: They'll sprout, but develop smaller than normal because of depleted food reserves. (With superior care, they may conceivably catch up with their siblings as they mature.)

Materials

☐ Experiment in progress from activity 5.
☐ Greenhouse from activity 9.

GROW, GROW, GROW

1 Make 4 more aluminum planters. Pack **brim full** with moist soil.

LEVEL!

LABEL

14A   14B   14C   14D

2 Poke a hole this deep into each planter. . .

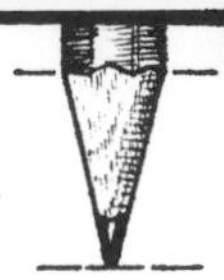

. . .then drop 2 radish seeds into each hole and cover with soil.

14A   14B   14C   14D

3 Stand the planters in your watering tray.

14A   14B   14C   14D

stop! stop! stop! stop! stop! stop! stop! stop! stop! stop!

return in 2 days:

4 Cut out the card below. Write your name(s) on it.

Cut EXACTLY ON THE LINE at the bottom of the ruler!

I get paid for this with radish sprouts!

5 Use this card for seedling measurement every day. Be sure to:

A Rest the "0" line squarely on the soil.

Mon.
Tues.

14A

B Bend the ruler to match the plant.

Never pull on the plant!

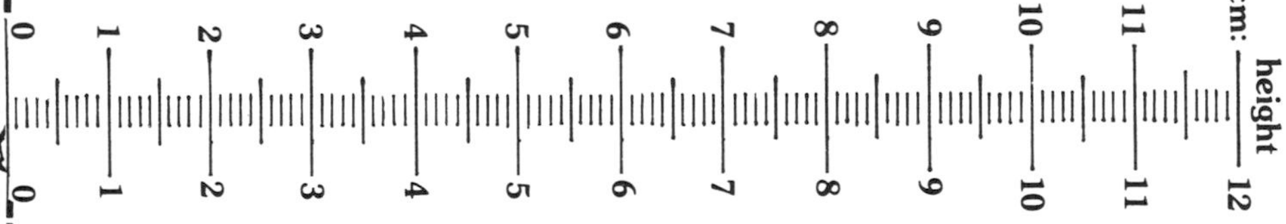

14A

C Measure to the nearest 0.1 cm.

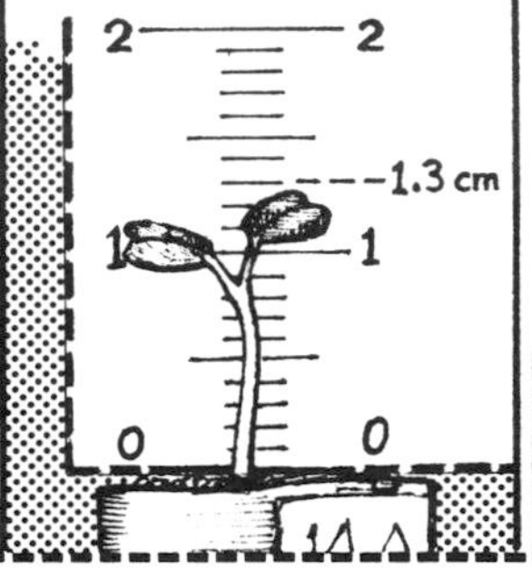

1.3 cm

14A

D Thin out the latecomers.

Sorry, just one sprout per planter.

14C

cm: height

name

GROW!

	Fri.	Sat.	Sun.	Mon.	Tues.	Wed.	Thur.	Fri.	Sat.	Sun.	Mon.	Tues.
HEIGHT 14A	0.0 cm											
14B	0.0 cm											
14C	0.0 cm											
14D	0.0 cm											

TOPS LEARNING SYSTEMS

Objective

To measure and record the growth in developing radish seedlings over an extended period of time.

Lesson Notes

1. See activity 2 for more detailed instructions on making foil mini-planters.

3. Your watering tray should now contain 10 planters, 6 from previous activities plus these 4 new ones.

4. Ask students to exercise extreme care as they cut across the bottom of the ruler. Cutting to either side of the line at this point will alter the zero point and bias the whole ruler.

5. All students need practice taking accurate measurements and recording data. Don't allow members of the same lab group to all use the same figures. One original set of measurements per student, please.

Procedures A, B and C require special emphasis. Students have a natural tendency to pull on the radish, making it conform to the height they think it should have! Don't even touch the plant, if possible. Rather, bend the ruler (zero point touching the surface of the soil) to match any phototropic leaning in the plant. Then read the ruler to the nearest 0.1 cm. Use decimals, not fractions. Don't round off to the nearest cm.

End your remarks with a demonstration. While your students look on, measure a radish from planter 2A or 2B. Be secretive about your answer. Write it on a slip of paper and put it in your pocket. Then challenge a volunteer to measure the same radish independently, staying within 0.3 cm of the measurement in your pocket.

Ask lab partners, in like manner, to also compare independent measurements. Values can disagree up to 0.3 cm due to random measuring error. Disagreements of more than 0.3 cm should be rechecked for student error.

Two radishes were originally planted in step 2, increasing the odds that a least one will sprout. Step 5D reminds you to thin out this second radish as soon as it sprouts. You can throw it away or transplant it (See activity 7, note 5).

Return every lab day, as the calendar suggests, to take 4 new measurements. To promote accuracy, remind lab partners to first measure independently, then compare answers. Record all data right next to the ruler in the table provided. This data will be plotted into sigma curves in activity 20.

Scheduling

Related Activities: 2---**14**---20.

Check Point

Do measurements agree among lab partners within the limits of random measuring error? Is each measurement expressed to the nearest 0.1 cm?

Model Answers

Measurements vary according to individual differences among radishes and growing conditions. Here is one typical result for one particular radish:

Fri — 0.0 cm
Mon — 0.1 cm
Tue — 1.2 cm
Wed — 2.7 cm
Thu — 4.0 cm
Fri — 6.0 cm
Mon — 7.4 cm
Tue — 7.9 cm

Materials

☐ Aluminum foil.
☐ A 4x6 index card.
☐ Scissors.
☐ Size-D battery, dead or alive.
☐ Tape.
☐ Moist potting soil.
☐ 8 radish seeds
☐ Watering tray from activity 2.

SUN SALAD

1 Pick a green seedling with bowed head from the four that you planted in the upper left corner of your greenhouse.

WARM DARK MOIST

WARM LIGHT MOIST

2 Taste these 3 parts:

All parts are good to eat!

Where's mine?

How do the green **COTYLEDONS** taste?

How does the pink **HYPOCOTYL** taste?

How does the white **TAP ROOT** taste?

Which part of the radish forms the vegetable you see in the store? Give **2 reasons** why you know for sure.

3 Radish leaves photosynthesize: Green chlorophyll turns the sun's energy into food energy (sugar).

Sun Energy

Sugar

Explain how radishes enable you to "eat" sun energy.

If all plants (including radishes) disappeared from the earth, could animals (including you) get energy? Explain.

TOPS LEARNING SYSTEMS

Objective

To determine what part of a radish seedling forms the commercial vegetable. To trace the flow of energy from the sun, through a radish, to you, the consumer.

Lesson Notes

1. Why select a green seedling with bowed head? It is during this brief stage of early development that the hypocotyl may reveal its first flush of radish pink. As the cotyledons lift and the hypocotyl lengthens, this coloration becomes masked by chlorophyll green. It will eventually turn red again, but several weeks later in the maturing process. If mold has begun to grow in the greenhouse, the sprouts should be rinsed in clean water before students eat them. Some students may be allergic to molds.

2. Eating your experiment does seem a bit unusual. Depending on the maturity of your age group, the first few students to taste their radishes may experience initial embarrassment. When a few more try it, so that radish tasting becomes an acceptable practice, watch out. Their zippy taste will make radish seedlings an extremely popular item. (Students we know actually sold them to classmates for a nickel apiece!)

Only the 4 radishes above the first circle should be eaten. All other radishes belong to other experiments in progress. They are strictly off limits.

The hypocotyl seems to have the right color and certainly the right taste. Why, then, does it have the wrong shape? Two reasons. First, it is far too immature. Farm-grown radishes are 3 weeks old, not 3 days old like these. Second, classroom growing conditions — lack of soil nutrients, minimum growing space, poor lighting — severely limit growth. Long and skinny may not look like much down on the farm, but in your classroom environment, it's the best they can grow. Anyway, they still taste right.

Scheduling

Related Activities: 9---**15**.

You must start this activity on time, but you can finish it later.

Model Answers

2. The COTYLEDONS taste mildly zippy.

The HYPOCOTYL tastes spicy hot.

The TAP ROOT tastes bland.

The hypocotyl forms the vegetable you see in the store. It is the only part with a radish pink color. And it has the zippiest radish taste.

3. Radishes enable you to "eat" the sun's energy because green chlorophyll in the radish leaves absorb this energy. They use sunlight to photosynthesize carbon dioxide and water into sugars that are then stored in the hypocotyl. When you eat this hypocotyl, your body digests the stored sugar, making it available as energy again.

If all plants (including radishes) disappeared from earth, all animals (including people) would starve to death for lack of energy. Unlike green plants, animals cannot photosynthesize their own food from sunlight. Animals get energy by eating plants (or other animals that have fed on plants). Green plants form the base of the food chain upon which all animal life depends.

Materials

☐ Greenhouse from activity 9.

TOXIC STRESS

1 Fold a paper towel in half 4 times to make 16 layers.

SECOND FOLD
FOURTH
THIRD
FIRST FOLD

2 Press a circle into the soft layers by pushing down firmly with the mouth of a baby food jar.

3 Cut around the circle impression. Push these 16 layers into the bottom of the jar.

4 Prepare 2 more jars like the first. Fill all 3 as directed, and label with tape:

• Soak layers with **WATER**.
• Drain excess.
• Add **8** radish seeds on top of the towels.

WATER

• Soak with **VINEGAR**.
• Drain excess.
• Add **4** radish seeds.

VINEGAR

• Mix 1 teaspoon **SALT** in a glass of water.
• Soak and drain.
• Add **4** radish seeds.

SALT WATER

5 Seal each jar with a lid. Set them aside on your index card.

WATER

stop! stop! stop! stop!

return in 9 days:

6 Can radishes grow in soils that are acidic or salty? Explain.

7 On the back of this page, write a brief report about one of these problems:

ACID RAIN
OR
EVAPORATION AND
SOIL SALINITY

TOPS LEARNING SYSTEMS

Objective

To expose radish seeds to acid and salt water. To appreciate that acid rain or soil salinity inhibit seed germination.

Lesson Notes

7. Both of these topics are briefly summarized in the class discussion below. Ask students to summarize the information you present. Or send them to the library to do more in-depth research.

A good place to find information about acid rain in the library is to look in the *Readers Guide to Periodical Literature*. Numerous magazine articles have been written about this important environmental issue. Begin research on soil salinity by looking in an encyclopedia under the topic "irrigation," then consult subheadings about "drainage." Or search for information on the world wide web.

Discussion

• **ACID RAIN:** Acid rain and snow occur when pollutants are released into the atmosphere from burning fossil fuels. Oxides of nitrogen and sulfur combine with water vapor in the atmosphere to form nitric and sulfuric acids, which then fall as rain and snow.

Acid rain collects in lakes and ponds, turning them more and more acidic. In time, populations of fish and other aquatic life diminish or disappear altogether. Hundreds of lakes in North America and Europe now no longer have any fish. Agriculture and forest productivity also suffer, but the effects are not as well understood or documented.

The radishes in this activity were subjected to full-strength vinegar. While vinegar illustrates the problem, it doesn't simulate actual conditions. Acid rain hasn't gotten that bad yet. Vinegar has roughly 100 times more acidity than dead lakes that no longer support fish. Dead lakes in turn have roughly 100 times more acidity than living lakes not yet affected by acid rain.

• **EVAPORATION AND SALINITY:** Polish a microscope slide with a clean paper towel. Put just one small drop of tap water on this slide and set it aside to evaporate. (A radiator or sunny window ledge will speed the process.) Pass the slide around your classroom to let students observe the dried spot. All this salt (dissolved minerals) in just 1 drop of drinking water!

Suppose we irrigate a field of radishes using water from the same source. Imagine how it might collect in the field, then evaporate, collect and evaporate, irrigation after irrigation, year after year. Over time, these minerals might accumulate to such a concentration that some future crop of radishes would grow poorly or hardly sprout at all.

What to do? Dig drainage ditches so some of the irrigation water can dissolve accumulating salts out of the soil and carry them off the field. (At this point rinse the salt deposit off the slide.)

Scheduling

Related Activities: **16** ---17---18.

You can do steps 3, 4 and 5 of activity 12 a day early. It's OK to finish this activity in less than 9 days.

Extension

Make a saturated solution of salt water: Add a large dose of table salt to water; shake well; allow the solution to settle; pour off clear brine, leaving excess salt behind. In a series of small jars, find the maximum concentrations of salt and vinegar in which radish seeds can successfully sprout. Dilute the original solutions of saturated salt and full strength vinegar successively in half (1:1, 1:2, 1:4, 1:8, 1:16, 1:32, etc.) until you find concentrations the radishes will tolerate. Knowing these rough limits, define maximum concentrations more precisely. This might turn into a great science project.

(We successfully sprouted radish seeds in white vinegar diluted to 1 part in 64, and in a saturated salt solution diluted to 1 part in 32.)

Model Answers

6. Radishes cannot grow in acidic or salty soils if the concentrations are too great. Only the radish seeds exposed to pure water sprouted. Those in the other two jars failed to germinate.

7. Reports will vary. See Discussion.

Materials

☐ Masking tape.
☐ Three baby food jars with lids.
☐ Table salt.
☐ A glass and a teaspoon.
☐ Vinegar.
☐ Paper towels.
☐ Scissors.

GEOTROPISM

1 Pick out a seedling with root hairs from the pure water jar of activity 16.

Root hairs!

2 Put about this much water in a baby food jar. . .

NOT ENOUGH TO SPILL OUT

. . .and put your seedling **head first** into the jar.

3 Slowly tip the jar upright so the seedling sticks to the glass side. It should be upside down and out of the water.

!

4 Close the lid. Push it on tight so water can't evaporate out.

?

5 Stick magic tape to the outside of the jar, then trace the seedling's outline onto the tape.

Then set the jar aside on your index card.

stop! stop! stop! stop! stop! stop! stop! stop! stop! stop! stop!

6 Draw how the plant grew over 24 hours.

BEFORE:

AFTER:

7 How does your seedling grow in response to gravity?

8 "Geotropism" means "earth-turning." It can be positive or negative.

NEGATIVE ↑ *turns AWAY from the earth.*

POSITIVE ↓ *turns TOWARD the earth.*

What part of your radish is **negatively** geotropic? Explain.

What part of your radish is **positively** geotropic? Explain.

TOPS LEARNING SYSTEMS

Objective

To observe how the root and hypocotyl of an upside-down radish seedling reorient in response to gravity. To distinguish between positive and negative geotropism.

Lesson Notes

3-4. The wet seedling is held to the side of the jar by the adhesion of water to glass. An airtight seal prevents the seedling from drying and falling to the bottom of the jar.

6. To avoid having to draw a "before" image of the seedling, some students may be tempted to remove the taped tracing and paste it directly into the first box of step 6. Don't allow this. By leaving the original "before" tracing taped to the jar, it is much easier to identify tropisms that have occurred in the live seedling superimposed underneath, and draw better comparison sketches.

8. If students experience difficulty here, review the vocabulary of tropisms presented in teaching notes 12.

Scheduling

Related Activities: 12---16---**17**---18.

After finishing this activity, you may begin activity 19.

Extension

(1) After completing activity 12, water the seedlings in planter 2C, then turn them on their side in the empty jar lid. Observe their growth response to this new orientation after one day.

(2) Decide whether the growth you observe is geotropic, phototropic, or both. Design an experiment to control the variables. (Grow the seedlings sideways in total darkness. A drawer, dark cupboard or closet should eliminate any phototropic response.)

Background

Shoots grow *up* because they are *negatively* geotropic; roots grow *down* because they are *positively* geotropic. Descriptions like these accurately define plant responses to specific stimuli. They sound scientific. But do they really explain anything fundamental? No. The complex whys and hows all remain unanswered.

It is beyond the scope of this book and the knowledge of this author to offer more fundamental explanations about plant physiology. Nevertheless, your students need to appreciate that the iceberg of scientific knowledge is huge, not for the knowns we see above the water, but for the unknowns that lay beneath. Let's take just a brief look at the waterline.

In recent years botanists have identified a plant hormone know as auxin that is responsible for many tropisms observed in plants. Auxin is produced in the growing tips of young seedlings and in the leaves, then transported to other growth zones where it acts to regulate the rate of cell elongation. Within limits, the more auxin that is present in a cell, the greater its elongation.

This discovery explains a great deal. The unequal distribution of auxin within a plant shoot causes one side to grow faster than the other. Unequal growth creates a curvature, a tropic plant response.

Plants are phototropic because light receptors in the shoot tip somehow initiate a chain of reactions that pump greater concentrations of auxin to the darker side of the shoot. If plants are totally in the dark, auxin concentrations increase on all sides, and the shoot grows rapidly straight up. (Remember the seedlings in the foil covered jar?)

Plants are geotropic because gravity concentrates auxin on the underside of shoots and roots. If a shoot is turned sideways, greater concentrations of auxin accumulate on the lower side, causing this part of the shoot to grow faster (curve up). The roots, which are more sensitive to auxin, are already growing at a maximum rate. If a root is turned sideways, the accumulated auxin on the lower side creates an overdose, causing this part of the root to grow slower (curve down).

Model Answers

6.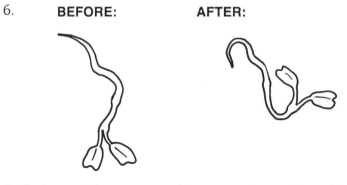

BEFORE: **AFTER:**

7. The hypocotyl grows upward in response to gravity, and the root tip grows downward.

8. The hypocotyl is negatively geotropic. It grows away from the earth.

The root tip is positively geotropic. It grows toward the earth.

Materials

☐ A young radish seedling germinating in the jar labeled "WATER" from activity 16.
☐ A baby food jar and lid.
☐ Clear tape that accepts pencil or pen markings.

HYDROTROPISM

1 Cut half a paper towel.

2 Fold it so one end hangs about 1/3 of the way down the outside of a baby food jar.

Moisten with water.

⅓ ⅓ ⅓

3 Cut a small piece of plastic so it exactly fits the overhanging towel.

Perfect fit!

4 Take 3 more seedlings with root hairs from the pure water jar of activity 16.

3 sprouts...

Gently place these **between** the towel and plastic:

Point roots **down**, just under the plastic.

COVER COMPLETELY with plastic.

5 Add water **no higher** than 1/2 full. **Gently** place a lid on the top.

WATER LOWER THAN TOWEL.

LOOSE LID

Set this aside on your index card.

stop! stop! stop! stop! stop! stop! stop! stop! stop! stop! stop! stop!

return in 6 days:

6 Draw how the roots grew when they reached dry glass.

WET TOWEL

DRY GLASS

7 HYDRO means WATER

Is a radish root **hydro**tropic? Explain, using "positive" or "negative" in your answer.

TOPS LEARNING SYSTEMS

Objective

To observe how radish roots grow in response to abrupt changes in moisture.

Lesson Notes

4. A total of 4 seedlings (3 from this activity, 1 from the last) have now been removed from the pure water jar in the toxic stress experiment. Those that remain serve as a standard of comparison for the seeds in the vinegar and salt water jars. Again, remember to reseal the lid after removing the seedlings.

5. Keep the water level inside the jar lower than the end of the towel that hangs outside. If the towel or its plastic covering dip below the waterline, it will siphon water from the jar.

Rest the lid loosely on the mouth of the jar. This reduces water lost to evaporation without restricting the flow of water through the overhanging towel.

Scheduling

Related Activities: 12---16---17---**18**.

Once it is clear how the roots respond, you can finish up. This might happen in less than 6 days.

Background

Roots grow at the tip. Cells multiply just behind the protective root cap in a region known as the meristem, then elongate and finally differentiate into the specialized cell structures of the mature root.

As root tips grow, they turn away from regions of low moisture and reach toward regions of higher moisture. But they can only do this by being in direct contact with moisture — by following the gradient toward a more abundant water source. Roots can't sense water across a dry barrier.

When roots reach areas that are water-rich, they branch and develop enormous numbers of root hairs to drink it up. If the supply becomes exhausted, roots will generally grow downward, responding to gravity, unless other moisture gradients lead in alternate directions.

Extension

Repeat this experiment, beginning with seeds instead of seedlings. Do young radicles respond differently than 3-day old tap roots? (Young radicles are more likely to take a U-turn back to the moist paper. However, the growing hypocotyl does the turning. The root remains an undeveloped nub.)

Model Answers

6. Radish roots typically respond to a dry boundary in one of the following three ways. One lab group seldom has sprouts that do all three. After they have recorded their results, you might survey the class as a whole to locate examples of each response. Encourage students to visit these other groups and observe their radishes.

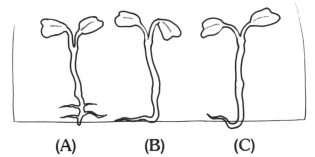

(A)   **(B)**   **(C)**

(A) It stops growing. Its cells no longer divide and elongate. An SOS goes out to the pericycle, a layer of undifferentiated cells higher up in the root. These cells begin to divide and elongate, creating lateral roots that branch out above the dry, dead primary root tip.

(B) It curves sideways, growing along the bottom edge of the towel. If the gradient from wet to dry is not too abrupt, the root tip can sense the increasing dryness and grow right or left before drying out.

(C) It does a U-turn back to the moist towel. There must be enough humidity evaporating from the moist towel for the root to "sense" its way back. (This behavior is more characteristic of very young seedlings. See Extension.)

7. A radish root is positively hydrotropic. It grows toward areas of greater moisture, either by bending at the tip or branching lateral roots.

Materials

☐ A paper towel.
☐ Scissors.
☐ A baby food jar with lid.
☐ Plastic wrap.
☐ Three young seedlings from the jar marked "WATER" in activity 16.

SEED LEAF OR TRUE?

1 Take planter **2B** from your watering tray.

2 There are 2 different kinds of leaves on your plants. Cut off one of each kind.

Cut with long stems.

3 Hold each leaf up to good light and carefully draw the pattern of veins you see.

Take time to draw careful details!

DRAW VEIN PATTERNS

COTYLEDON

TRUE LEAF

4 Put each leaf on a smooth surface. Lay these boxes over the correct leaf, and shade **gently** with the side of your pencil lead.

DON'T SQUASH ME!

RUBBING:

MAKE A RUBBING

COTYLEDON:

TRUE LEAF:

5 List all the differences you can see between the cotyledon and the true leaf.

SIZE? AGE? COLOR? SHAPE? EDGES? VEINS? THICKNESS? TEXTURE ???

6 What's different about the birth of the cotyledons and the birth of true leaves? Explain in words and pictures.

Finish your answers on the back.

TOPS LEARNING SYSTEMS

Objective

To compare cotyledons with true leaves according to structure, function and origin.

Lesson Notes

2. Only "teenage" radishes have both kinds of leaves. They are old enough to have well developed true leaves, but not so old that the cotyledons have already withered and died.

The radishes in 2B should be about the right age. But if you find the cotyledons are too shrivelled and yellow, choose one from a younger seedling. Radishes in 2C are 10 days younger.

3. Contrast the simple pattern of veins on the cotyledon with the complex network on the true leaf. Your students will need good light, good eyesight, and a good deal of patience. They may not have the persistence to draw veins on a whole leaf, but should complete at least a section of it in careful detail. Distribute hand lenses if available.

Here is a good place to introduce the vocabulary of primary, secondary and tertiary veins. Ask students to find examples of each and label them.

4. Emphasize that leaf rubbings require a light touch. You can demonstrate the consequences of pressing too hard: first the leaf cells break, then the paper absorbs moisture; then the pencil lead digs through the wet paper, leaving a hole.

Younger children probably won't capture much detail, especially on the cotyledons. But rubbings are fun, and your students may want to experiment with other kinds of leaves, coins, and textured surfaces, such as fabrics. Consider asking them to practice on other objects before they try radish parts.

Cheaper, thinner, rougher paper, with lighter pencil pressure, will actually work better for the tiny, fragile radish leaves. You might hand out small pieces of thin paper (semi-opaque tracing paper works well); rubbings can be then be taped on the activity pages. Older students can try using the point of a pencil *very lightly* for the best possible detail.

6. Students who experience difficulty here need to be reminded how the cotyledons develop from the original seed. Refer them to the sprout drawings they made way back in activity 3.

Scheduling

Related Activities: 2---**19**.
It's OK to finish this activity later than scheduled.

Background

A seed is made of three basic parts: an embryo, a source of stored food, and a seed coat. In the radish seed, the stored food is actually attached to and folded around the rest of the living embryo. It dominates the embryo inside. Hello, cotyledons!

As the seed germinates and the embryo grows, the unfolding cotyledons begin to dispense their food reserves. Before supplies run out, however, these clever cotyledons switch from being food storehouses to food producers. They turn green and begin to photosynthesize, just like true leaves.

They continue to convert water and carbon dioxide into sugar (with the help of the sun's energy) until true leaves develop. Once new leaves are well established, the old cotyledons gracefully retire. They slowly lose their chlorophyll, turn yellow, and wither to brown nothings that drop from the plant.

Model Answers

3.

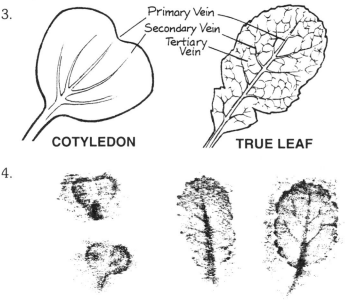

COTYLEDON   TRUE LEAF

Primary Vein
Secondary Vein
Tertiary Vein

4.

5. This is a great exercise in learning to make comparisons. Students may observe other differences besides the ones listed here. They'll need to use the back of their papers.

a. Size: The true leaf is larger than the cotyledon (unless the leaf has not yet fully developed.)

b. Color: The cotyledon is a paler green, tending toward yellow; the true leaf is a darker green. (This yellowness is characteristic of beginning atrophy in the aging cotyledon.)

c. Shape: A cotyledon is somewhat heart-shaped; a true leaf is more oval with occasional indentations.

d. Age: The cotyledons were present in the original seed. They are older than the true leaf.

e. Edges: Cotyledons have smooth edges; the true leaf is saw-toothed and somewhat convoluted.

f. Veins: Two sets of secondary veins emerge from one primary vein in the cotyledon. The true leaf has a more complex network: secondary veins branch from a central primary vein; tertiary veins branch from the secondaries.

g. Thickness: A cotyledon is thicker, more fleshy and firmer; a true leaf is thinner, less substantial.

h. Texture: A cotyledon is smooth and hairless; a true leaf is covered with tiny barb-like hairs.

6. The cotyledons are part of the original seed. (Students should refer to growth stages B and C in activity 3.)

The true leaves begin to develop after 2 weeks, and soon grow much larger than the original cotyledons. (Students should refer to their 2 WEEK grid sketch in activity 10.)

Materials

☐ Watering tray from activity 2.
☐ Scissors.
☐ A hand lens (optional).

GROW GRAPHS

1 Plot all height measurements from your **GROW!** card (activity 14) onto each graph below.

PLOT DATA

CIRCLE POINTS

SEEDLING 14 A:

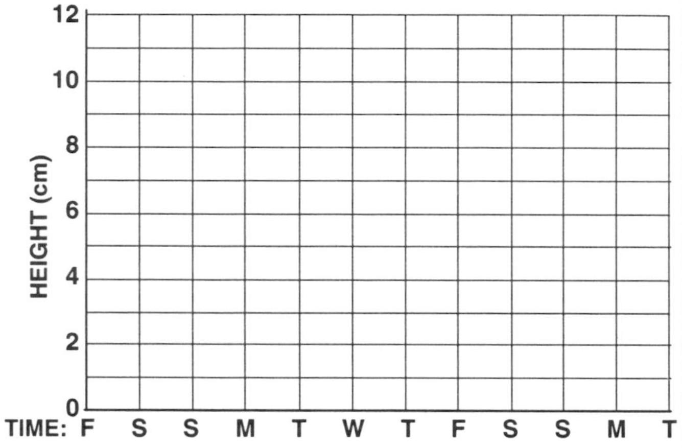

HEIGHT (cm)

12 · 10 · 8 · 6 · 4 · 2 · 0

TIME: F S S M T W T F S S M T

SEEDLING 14 B:

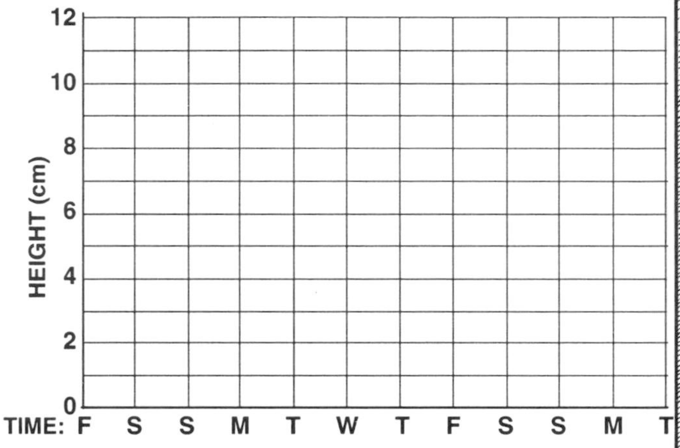

HEIGHT (cm)

12 · 10 · 8 · 6 · 4 · 2 · 0

TIME: F S S M T W T F S S M T

SEEDLING 14 C:

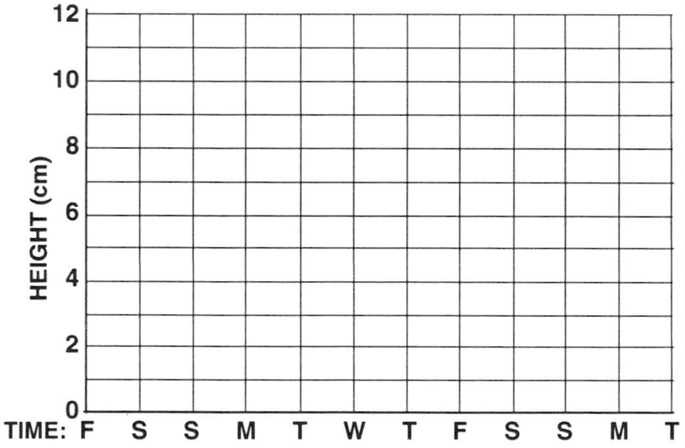

HEIGHT (cm)

12 · 10 · 8 · 6 · 4 · 2 · 0

TIME: F S S M T W T F S S M T

SEEDLING 14 D:

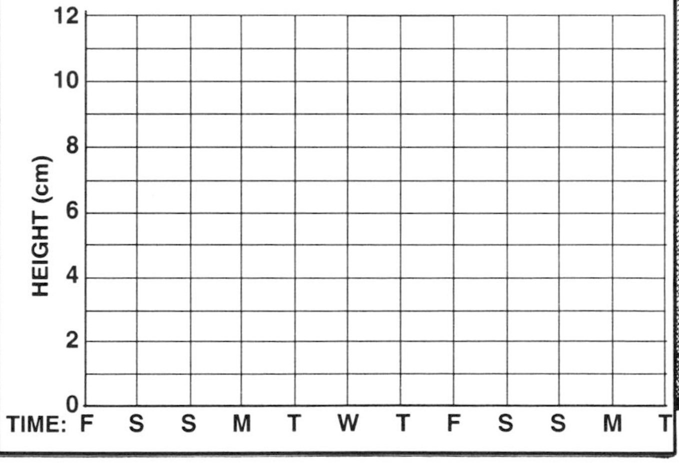

HEIGHT (cm)

12 · 10 · 8 · 6 · 4 · 2 · 0

TIME: F S S M T W T F S S M T

2 Draw the best smooth **sigma curves** you can for each graph. Don't draw inside your circles.

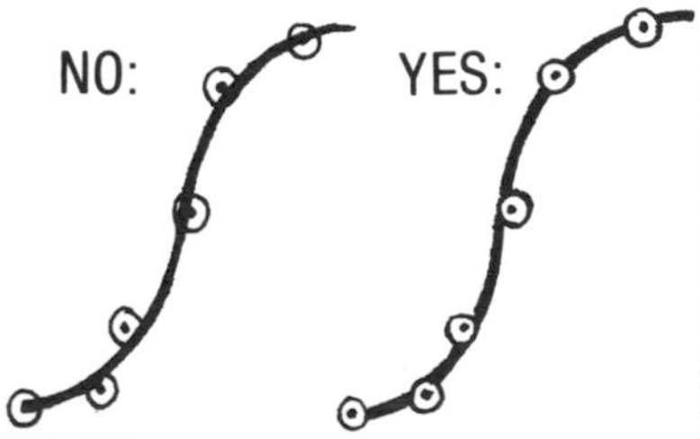

NO: YES:

3 Tell how fast your seedlings grew through each part of the curve.

Bottom of curve:

Middle of curve:

Top of curve:

TOPS LEARNING SYSTEMS

Objective

To graph the data collected in activity 14. To interpret radish growth in terms of a sigma curve.

Lesson Notes

The growth of a single cell, a stem, or even a whole plant, doesn't proceed at a constant rate, even under uniform growing conditions. Growth starts slowly, gradually increases to a maximum rate, then falls off and finally stops.

Plotting any size variable (height, weight, etc.) on the vertical axis against time on the horizontal axis, results in a typical sigma curve. Sudden changes in temperature or other ambient conditions may cause local fluctuations in a particular data point, but the overall S-shape remains.

1-2. Your class has already plotted a sprout graph with a similar S-curve. If necessary, review the process of circling scattered data points, and drawing smooth curves. (See step 2 of Teaching Notes 8.)

The bottom of the curve is not as flat as the data seems to indicate. Remember that the seeds grew roughly 2 cm (the length of a pencil point) just to reach the zero-point on each graph. Taking this underground growth into account creates a more idealized S-shape.

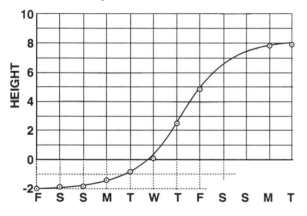

Scheduling

Related Activities: 2---14---**20**.

It's OK to finish this activity later.

Extension

Bell curves are closely related to sigma curves. Let's see how they compare. First copy this data table. It represents the growth pattern for an idealized plant.

DAY	TOTAL HEIGHT (CM)	DAILY INCREASE (CM)
FRI	0.0	
SAT	0.1	
SUN	0.3	
MON	0.7	
TUES	1.5	
WED	3.1	
THURS	6.3	
FRI	7.9	
SAT	8.7	
SUN	9.1	
MON	9.3	
TUES	9.4	

Fill in the column on the right with the increase in height for each day. Then get an extra Grow Graphs worksheet and plot each column of data on a separate graph.

Notice how a sigma curve tracks height *totals* for each day; a bell curve tracks height *increases* for each day.

Model Answers

1. Here is a typical graph result. Students should draw 4 similar graphs, one for each seedling.

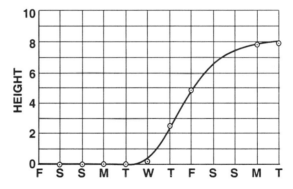

3. Bottom of curve: Slow growth in the beginning.
   Middle of curve: Rapid growth during this middle period.
   Top of curve: Slow growth later on.

Materials

☐ Height measurements from activity 14.

DRAWING GRID

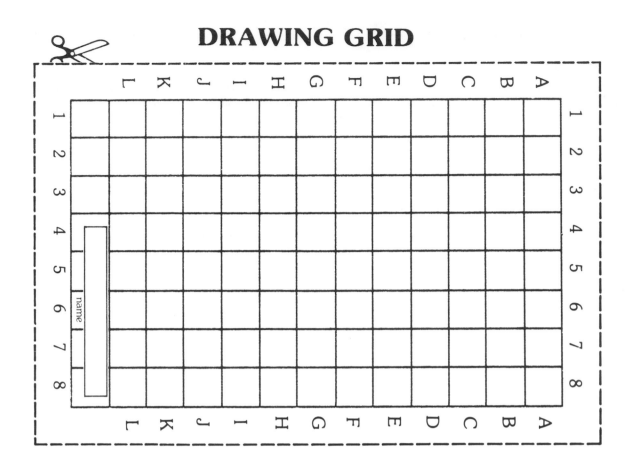

DRAWING GRID

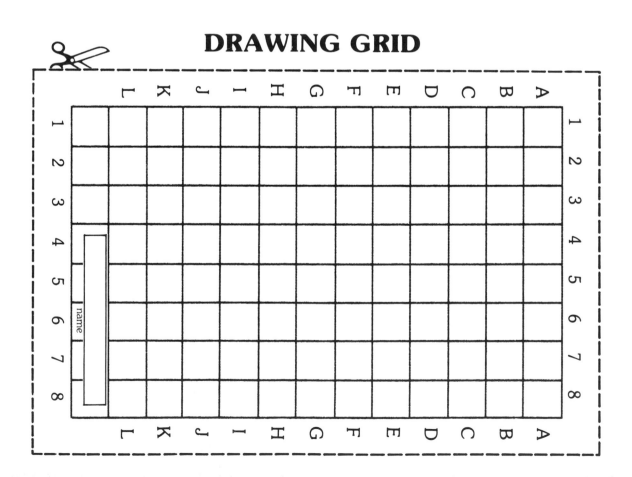

Feedback!

Dear Educator,

If you enjoyed teaching TOPS, please say so. Your praise will motivate us to work harder. If you found an error or can suggest ways to improve this program, we need to hear about that too. Your criticism will help us improve our next new edition. Do you need information about our other publications? We'll send you our latest catalog free of charge.

For whatever reason, we'd love to hear from you, and will carefully consider your input. We include this self-mailer for your convenience.

Sincerely,

Ron & Peg

Ron and Peg Marson
author and illustrator

module title _____   date _____

name _____

address _____

city _____ state _____ zip_____

FIRST FOLD

SECOND FOLD

RETURN ADDRESS

_____

_____

_____

PLACE
STAMP
HERE

TOPS Learning Systems
10970 S. Mulino Road
Canby OR 97013

TAPE HERE